H

THE PURE LIFE

A Smart Guide for Food and Nutrition for a Healthy Lifestyle from the Quran and Hadith

Ayatullah Sayyid Muhammad Taqi al-Modarresi

Commentary by
Zainali Panjwani and Jaffer Ladak

The Pure Life

Ayatullah Sayyid Muhammad Taqi al-Modarresi
With Commentary by Zainali Panjwani and Jaffer Ladak

ISBN: 978-1-927930-31-1
First Published in 2022 by Islamic Publishing House - www.iph.ca

Cover Design and Text Layout
Shaykh Saleem Bhimji for Islamic Publishing House

Contents

Dedication

Please recite a Surah al-Fatiha for the reward of the following individuals:

Marhum Aqeel Hasan Noorali

Marhuma Masooma Nisar

Marhumeen of Ali Abdulhussein Albaker Family

Marhum Syed Sabir Shah and all Marhumeen of the Family

Marhumeen of Abdurasul Muraj, Sumar Families and Dr. Gulamhusein Peermohamed Families

Marhum Mohamedjaffer KG and Marhuma Fatmabai KG

Marhum Nabil Bairam

Marhum Abbas Ali Jaffry and Sharaf Ilahi Abbas

Marhuma Abida Parveen

Marhum Rawji Jessa and Family

Marhumeen of the Nasser (Mamado) Family

Marhoom Syed Asad Ali Rizvi, Marhoom Syeda Shahida Begum, Marhoom Syed Muhammad Raza Jaffery and Marhoom Syeda Jaffery

Marhoom Raza Dewji

Marhumeen HuseinAli HassanAli Jeevraj and Family

Marhum Azadali Jafferali Kassam
Marhum Mohamed-Taki Gulamali Somji

Syeda Nasim Jaffri Shah, Syed Shabbir Hussain Shah, Syeda Umay Farwa and all marhumeen of the Jaffri Family

Marhumeem of Ased Ali and Shafaq Hussain-Ali Families

Marhum Meraj Rasool ibn Abdul Ghaffar Sheikh

Hajj Karim Alarakhia

Introduction

Eating is not just about how appealing the food looks, how tasty it is or how many calories it contains. Food is medicine and enrichment for the body. It is unique coding and information for the different processes that are required for us to function optimally, physically and spiritually. What we consume, how we consume it and who we consume it with have profound impacts on the soul of a human being.

What most people never come to realise is how corporations have mastered the engineering of food production, advertising and keeping people addicted to the unhealthiest of lifestyles. What has become normal has only become "normalised" by the overriding cultures of greed and excess that we have been born into and thus cyclically contribute toward, just as Prophet Muhammad ﷺ said: "What I fear most for you is the capricious appetites that will, from your stomachs and private parts, lead you astray."[1]

The lifestyles we choose to live individually become part of the familial structure as much as the familial practises that reproduce our individual habits; these then become part of societal standards and necessarily replicate themselves for others to follow. These collective habits then become generational without people knowing exactly why they act as they do.

For this reason, Allah ﷻ tells us that He has provided us with ways of living, that are in conformity to His lofty path:

﴿وَلَقَدْ مَكَّنَّاكُمْ فِي الْأَرْضِ وَجَعَلْنَا لَكُمْ فِيهَا مَعَايِشَ قَلِيلًا مَّا تَشْكُرُونَ ﴿١٠﴾﴾

And certainly We have given you power in the earth, and We have made the ways of living for you in it, (but) little it is that you give thanks." (7:10)

From the Qur'anic persepctive, the ways of living may be divided into three:

1. That Which is Prohibited

As for the forbidden, Allah ﷻ gives an example of a set of prohibitions particularly to those of adult age, beginning their responsibilities, such as with a family or in the world of work: "Do not squander your wealth; do not kill your children in fear of poverty; do not approach fornication; do not usurp; do not cheat; do not follow what you do not have knowledge of; and do not strut about the earth arrogantly." This series of verses (17:23-37) ends with:

﴿كُلُّ ذَٰلِكَ كَانَ سَيِّئُهُ عِندَ رَبِّكَ مَكْرُوهًا ﴿٣٨﴾﴾

All of this is evil and detested in your Lord's sight. (17:38)

This tells us there are ways of living that are abhorred and impermissible with Allah ﷻ because our pursuance of them would be detrimental to our souls.

2. That Which is Permissible

Allah ﷻ has empowered mankind to have freedoms and amongst

them is to live a life which is rooted in practising that which is permissible and right. This is the base line, minimal expectations of how we live, which is to not contravene God's beautiful laws for: "Whoever honours the sacred rites of Allah, for him it is good." (22:30)

3. That Which is Pure, Lofty and Divine

The third is within the permissible but distinguished between what is merely allowed and what is choicest and ideal, pure and blessed. It is the opportunity of taking a higher course in all that we do; it is in fact, to live a godly life, as He ﷻ says:

﴿كُونُواْ رَبَّانِيِّينَ ... بِمَا كُنتُمْ تَدْرُسُونَ ۝٧٩﴾

> Become godly ... by virtue of your own deep study [of the religion]. (3:79)

To live such a life is referred to in the Qur'an as *Hayaatun Tayyibah*:

﴿مَنْ عَمِلَ صَالِحًا مِّن ذَكَرٍ أَوْ أُنثَىٰ وَهُوَ مُؤْمِنٌ فَلَنُحْيِيَنَّهُ
حَيَاةً طَيِّبَةً وَلَنَجْزِيَنَّهُمْ أَجْرَهُم بِأَحْسَنِ مَا كَانُواْ يَعْمَلُونَ ۝٩٧﴾

> As for anyone - be it man or woman - who does righteous deeds, and is a believer We will most certainly cause him to live a pure and blessed life. And most certainly shall We grant unto such as these their reward in accordance with the best that they ever did. (16:97)

In several verses does Allah ﷻ differentiate *halaal*, the merely permissible, and *tayyib*, the pure, lofty and ideal:

﴿يَا أَيُّهَا النَّاسُ كُلُواْ مِمَّا فِي الأَرْضِ حَلاَلاً طَيِّباً وَلاَ تَتَّبِعُواْ

خُطُوَاتِ الشَّيْطَانِ إِنَّهُ لَكُمْ عَدُوٌّ مُّبِينٌ ﴿١٦٨﴾

O Mankind! Partake of what is lawful and good on earth, and follow not Satan's footsteps: for, verily, he is your open foe. (2:168)

﴿وَكُلُواْ مِمَّا رَزَقَكُمُ اللَّهُ حَلَالًا طَيِّبًا وَاتَّقُواْ اللَّهَ الَّذِىَ أَنتُم بِهِ مُؤْمِنُونَ ﴿٨٨﴾

Thus, partake of the lawful, good things which God grants you as sustenance, and be conscious of God, in whom you believe. (5:88)

﴿فَكُلُواْ مِمَّا غَنِمْتُمْ حَلَالًا طَيِّبًا وَاتَّقُواْ اللَّهَ إِنَّ اللَّهَ غَفُورٌ رَّحِيمٌ ﴿٦٩﴾

Enjoy, then, all that is lawful and good among the things which you have gained in war, and remain conscious of God: verily, God is much-forgiving, a dispenser of grace. (8:69)

﴿فَكُلُواْ مِمَّا رَزَقَكُمُ اللَّهُ حَلَالًا طَيِّبًا وَاشْكُرُواْ نِعْمَتَ اللَّهِ إِن كُنتُمْ إِيَّاهُ تَعْبُدُونَ ﴿١١٤﴾

So partake of all the lawful, good things which God has provided for you as sustenance, and render thanks unto God for His blessings, if it is [truly] Him that you worship. (16:114)

In looking at these verses in their aggregate, one can see that *tayyib* is linked to the sustenance that Allah ﷻ provides, which means that He ﷻ always provides means to reach and partake in what is *tayyib* such that it leaves us without excuse to not elevate our lives to *Hayyatun Tayyibah*.

What is most interesting is that when referring to *tayyib*, this greater aspiration of discipline and awareness in lifestyle, Allah ﷻ proclaims that this is the realm of the Prophets, Messengers and Ahl al-Bayt ﵌ - yet at the same time lays an expectation upon the believers, ordinary people, that they too should be living the same lifestyle, *Hayaatun Tayyibah*, as did the Prophets!

He ﷻ addresses His Messengers saying:

﴿يَا أَيُّهَا الرُّسُلُ كُلُوا مِنَ الطَّيِّبَاتِ وَاعْمَلُوا صَالِحًا إِنِّي بِمَا تَعْمَلُونَ عَلِيمٌ ﴿٥١﴾﴾

O Messengers, eat of the pure things and do good. I know all that you do. (23:51)

Yet Allah ﷻ also addresses the believers to accord to the same, pure and lofty lifestyle!

﴿يَا أَيُّهَا الَّذِينَ آمَنُوا كُلُوا مِن طَيِّبَاتِ مَا رَزَقْنَاكُمْ وَاشْكُرُوا لِلَّهِ إِن كُنتُمْ إِيَّاهُ تَعْبُدُونَ ﴿١٧٢﴾﴾

Believers, eat the good things we provided you, and thank God, if you are truly worshiping Him. (2:172)

This is not the only time Allah ﷻ expects the ordinary believer to live and worship like the Prophets and Ahl al-Bayt ﵌. For example, in the verse encouraging the purpose of fasting, Allah ﷻ states:

﴿يَا أَيُّهَا الَّذِينَ آمَنُوا كُتِبَ عَلَيْكُمُ الصِّيَامُ كَمَا كُتِبَ عَلَى

ٱلَّذِينَ مِن قَبۡلِكُمۡ لَعَلَّكُمۡ تَتَّقُونَ ﴿١٨٣﴾

> O You who believe! Fasting is ordained for you as it was ordained for those before you so that you might remain conscious of God. (2:183)

According to a sound narration, none of the previous nations had the obligation of fasting. Rather, the meaning of this verse is that fasting was obligated on the Prophets of those nations and that the same fasting Muslims engage in, is a gift bestowed only upon the nation of the Prophet Muhammad ﷺ:

Imam as-Sadiq ﵇ said: "The month of Ramadan is not something Allah ﷻ made obligatory on any individual from the previous nations to us." The above verse was read to the Imam as a response. The Imam replied: "Allah ﷻ only made obligatory the fast of the month of Ramadan upon the Prophets, not their nations. So, Allah ﷻ graced it to this nation and made the fast upon the Messenger of Allah ﷺ and upon his community."[2]

This expectation of Allah ﷻ upon us to raise our standards of living to that of the Prophets is something truly inspiring! By placing such confidence in the Muslim, it demands of us to look into all areas of our life, the way we organise our time, what we purchase, how we keep company with people, our preparation of sleep, the items in our house - and ensure that they are not just *halaal* and what may be permissible, but rather what is lofty and pure, *tayyib*. In this way we would be living *Hayaatun Tayyibah.*

Translating the Work of Grand Ayatollah Syed Mohammed Taqi al-Modarresi

The body of this work is a translation from a chapter of the book

Hayaatun Tayyibah by Grand Ayatollah Syed Mohammed Taqi al-Modarresi, the *Marja'* (leading religious authority)[3] of the holy city of Kerbala, Iraq.

His work is considered to be 'a new page in *Fiqh*' (Islamic religious laws) which seeks to interrogate what are the various features of life that would, together, make up living a wholesome, holistic life. This ranges from principles of building state institutions such as healthcare and education systems, to how to organise the home, to the chapter which has been translated for this work, on food, consumption and table habits, the foundation of a pure and wholesome life.

The methodology of Ayatollah al-Modarresi is distinctive, maybe even unique, as can be noted by the translation.

A lifetime of dedication to the holy Qur'an has allowed him to seamlessly bring together verses regarding subjects, and with the sacred Prophetic narrations, extrapolate deep insights for the believer to benefit from.

In each section you will see a plethora of verses regarding the theme being studied followed by the sound narrations. Al-Modarresi puts these together like a jigsaw puzzle revealing the fullness of its picture and then draws from these *basa'ir*, or insights and from there the rulings that are to be followed. He refers to this practise as *tadabbur* or deeply pondering over the Qur'an.

Whilst all scholars privilege the Qur'an and Prophetic narrations, it is al-Modarresi's commitment to the Qur'an as the guiding light, building off its certainty and utilising the *'aql* - Divinely gifted and strengthened intellect - that make his approach so rare in the Muslim world.

Why was the Chapter of Food Translated?

The question of *what* we are is as important as who we are. What we are must also be answered by *'What are we made of?'*; the materials, energies and even processes that go into obtaining and feeding ourselves ultimately determine *what* we are.

Most people do not comprehend that we live in a completely unjust production, supply and consumption system, of which food is the central element to this.

As an example, a most important study undertaken on nutrition was the *China Study* by father and son researchers T. C. and T. M. Campbell, looking at the relationship between consumption and disease, meaning diet and long-term health.[4] [5]

Amongst the outcomes was the proposed shifting of the food pyramid, moving meat and dairy away from central and excess consumption owing to the vast array of diseases that were evidenced from their consumption.[6]

Despite the science providing this insight, pressure from meat and dairy lobbyists and corporations influenced the U.S. Department of Agriculture to withdraw its Eating Right Pyramid food guide not only influencing dietary recommendations but demonstrating that science and health is subservient to the almighty dollar.[7]

How many a hundred of millions of people has this affected?

According to Prophet Muhammad ﷺ such a system in which we are consuming that which is ruinous for the body will dull the senses, make people lazy in seeking the truth and lazy in their actions such that obesity would become prevalent.

What is interesting is that according to narrations, this state of people is a sign of the end of time, as he ﷺ is narrated to have said: "There will come a people, they will prefer watching and being idle and not dying for a cause, they will prefer betraying over being trustworthy; rampant obesity will appear in them [as a consequence]."[8]

One of the most important - and threatening to the corporate machine - findings, in the China Study was in regions where protein intake was less than 5% from meat and dairy, there was no cancer. This finding was replicated across the world from India to China with the same outcomes.

In well-known narrations, Prophet Muhammad ﷺ condemned excess intake of meat and himself would go a whole month without eating meats. For example, A'isha the wife of the Prophet ﷺ said: "We in the household of Muhammad ﷺ, used to live for a whole month without cooking anything over a fire."[9]

This is why Allah ﷻ warned not to turn lawful things into that which is abominable by committing excess: "O you who believe! Make not unlawful the good things, which Allah hath made lawful for you, and commit no excess, for Allah loves not those given to excess." (5:87)

If Allah ﷻ has made lawful the consumption of meat and dairy, why could it be leading to disease?

We may need to reflect on the idea that as a society trying to consume excess amounts of these food groups leads to unethical, unhealthy and poisonous farming methods which ultimately journeys through the food chain, affecting our bodies and the environment.

The nutrients that humans gain from consuming these foods are beneficial, as they provide a great source of essential amino acids, healthy fats, minerals and vitamins. However, are there alternatives to being able to consume a level of meat and dairy that is healthy for us and at the same time not damaging to our environment? We are, as a global community, now becoming more aware of a concept known as regenerative farming which allows for a renewed approach to healthy eating and protecting the environment.

As we can see from the above, the entire food cycle from production to lobbying, from consumption to recycling, and from material to the spiritual is entirely co-dependent; all of it combine to determining the central part of a truly Islamic lifestyle.

Hayatun Tayyibah and the book bearing its namesake, was a prime opportunity to provide guidance and support from the Islamic perspective on a topic that is becoming ever-more urgent; the physical-spiritual health of the Muslim community.

It is a space that combines the religious treasures embedded in our texts with the latest scientific understandings which are often too disparate and technical to make sense of.

Ten out of the top twenty-six countries that lead the body mass index (2014) are Muslim majority countries.

Islam's most sanctified sites have become 'junk-food fests'; McDonald's and other leading fast food outlets surround Islam's holiest location, Mecca's Masjid al-Haram offering toxic food to pilgrims before, during and after their worship, while the Al-Waha Company Coca Cola factory sits in Hilla, on the road between holy Najaf and Kerbala.

All of this continues to normalise the Muslim toward gorging on what is not only killing their spirituality but destroying their minds and bodies, or what Sheikh Hamza Yusuf refers to as consumption of "demonic calories."

This book therefore aims at being a small gesture toward an intervention - something that becomes necessary when a person can no longer control themselves. It is a attempt to disrupt the hegemony of our fast food and binge eating culture, to remind our communities of the relationship between God, food, the acts involved in eating, nourishment and the energies we gain from this process, both immediately and along the lifelong journey.

What is unique about this book?

This work has two ranges of commentary supplementing the translation of al-Modarresi's work. One is brief and found in the footnotes which aim to compliment the core text. These will be verses of the holy Qur'an and narrations that expand on a matter or in places draw together deeper insights that al-Modarresi has spoken about elsewhere.

For example, in his lecture series commenting on Chapter 56 of the Qur'an, Surah al-Waqi'ah, he reflects on the order of food served in paradise and from this extrapolates the order in which food should be served and eaten in this world. This is because paradise is of course, the perfect resort and so by priority is a lesson for us in this world.

Adding to this, the supplications Prophet Muhammad ﷺ made when laying and cleaning the dining table and other such narrations, the book provides a start to finish guide on the Prophetic model of eating, not seen in other books.

The book also explores one of the most important contemporary issues in purchasing and consumption practices since the start of the Covid-19 pandemic, hoarding and monopolising of essential foods. This section has been translated from the work *Fiqh as-Sadiq* of Ayatollah Mohammed Jawed Mughniyyah and contributes to the goal of al-Modarresi's work, which is to build a comprehensive and pure way of living.

The second form of commentary aims to expand on some of the concepts Ayatollah al-Moderresi has discussed and relate them to the physical realities of our life and the inner workings of our human body, dovetailing the traditional texts with the latest scientific studies.

Health is not just the absence of disease, it is a state of complete physical, mental and social well-being (1). In this commentary, we specifically seek to discuss how the impact of what we put into our bodies influences us physically, mentally and even socially.

These discussions are aimed at bringing an awareness to the way in which we choose to lead our lives and asks us to ponder on the relationship between our metaphysical soul and physical body. If what I consume can have such a profound impact on the overall health of the body, could it mean that the choices on what we eat and how we eat, be extremely influential to the journey of our souls? We will explore this question from a number of nutritional and scientific angles.

Ultimately this book is a reflection of a most profound narration by Imam Musa al-Kadhim ﷺ who stated: "Diet control is the fountainhead of remedies and the stomach is the house of all ailments, so condition your body while it can be conditioned."[10]

In bringing these two worlds, the traditional Islamic and scientific together, we sought to be an example of bridging a much-needed gap, both generally across the disciplines and specifically in nutritional research.

Throughout the book you will notice reflective questions and practical tips boxes. The aim being to help encourage lifestyle changes. The side space available can be used for annotation and note taking for further reflection.

It cannot be stressed enough the need for co-authorship amongst Muslim scholars from varied fields of knowledge which can provide an intersection of expertise built on the foundation of Islam. This urgently needs to become a standard in the Muslim world where ethical, psychological, economic, environmental and medical sciences challenge traditional Muslim scholarship and vice versa, bringing the best out of them together.

There is of course a great difference between calling for this and undertaking it, hence this work is written in one voice, for the words are a combination of research, discussions and mutual learning.

Special thanks goes to Sister Mariam Kourani for editing the Arabic translation, Sister Sajeda Sajan for her feedback on the manuscript, Sister Sumayya Pirbhai Ladak for her designs, and Shaykh Saleem Bhimji for bringing this work to fruition. Your rewards are with Allah ﷻ.

Zainali Panjwani and Jaffer Ladak
Muharram 1444
September 2022

Endnotes

1 This hadith is found in the Musnad of Abi Barzah al-Aslami, tradition 3,251. The Arabic text states:

إِنَّمَا أَخْشَى عَلَيْكُمْ شَهَوَاتِ الْغَيِّ فِي بُطُونِكُمْ وَفُرُوجِكُمْ وَمُضِلَّاتِ الْهَوَى

2 The Arabic text states:

سَمِعتُ أبا عَبدِ اللّه عليه السلام يَقولُ : إنَّ شهرَ رَمَضانَ لَم يَفرِضِ اللّهُ صِيامَهُ على أحَدٍ من الاُمَمِ قَبلَنا، فَقلتُ لَهُ : فقولُ اللّه عَزَّ و جلَّ : يا أيُّها الذين آمَنُوا كُتِبَ عَلَيكُمُ الصِّيامُ كَما كُتِبَ عَلَى الّذينَ مِن قَبلِكُم؟! قالَ: إنّما فَرَضَ اللّهُ صيامَ شَهرِ رَمَضانَ على الأنبياءِ دُونَ الاُمَمِ، فَفَضَّلَ اللّهُ بهِ هذهِ الاُمَّةَ، و جَعَلَ صيامَهُ فَرضا على رسولِ اللّهِ صلى الله عليه و آله و على اُمَّتِهِ

3 www.almodarresi.com/books/243/am0s6dkw.htm

4 https://www.researchgate.net/publication/245624911_The_China_Study_The_Most_Comprehensive_Study_of_Nutrition_Ever_Conducted_and_the_Startling_Implications_for_Diet_Weight_Loss_and_Long-Term_Health_Two_ReviewsThe_China_Study_The_Most_Comprehensive_Stud

5 The China Study, Campbell & Campbell, BenBella Books, 2006

6 https://nutritionstudies.org/solving-food-pyramid-mysteries/

7 https://pubmed.ncbi.nlm.nih.gov/8375951/

8 Al-Bukhari, The Book of Witnessing, trad. 2,651.

9 Sahih Muslim, The Book of Zuhd, trad. 2,792. The Arabic text states:

إِنْ كُنَّا آلَ مُحَمَّدٍ صَلَّى اللَّهُ عَلَيْهِ وَسَلَّمَ لَنَمْكُثُ شَهْرًا مَا نَسْتَوْقِدُ بِنَارٍ إِنْ هُوَ إِلَّا التَّمْرُ وَالْمَاءُ

10 Makarim al-Akhlaq, Vol. 2, Pg. 180, Trad. 2,468. The Arabic text states:

الحِميةُ رأسُ الدواءِ، والمَعِدةُ بيتُ الداءِ، عَوِّدْ بَدَناً ما تَعَوّدَ

Personal Notes

Biography

Grand Ayatollah as-Sayyid Mohammed Taqi al-Modarresi was born in 1945 in the holy city of Kerbala to a scholastic family. His father was Ayatollah as-Sayyid Muhammad Kadhim al-Modarresi, his mother was the daughter of Grand Ayatollah as-Sayyid Mahdi as-Shirazi and his uncle Grand Ayatollah as-Sayyid Mohammed Hussaini as-Shirazi.

Ayatollah al-Modarresi began his religious education in the religious seminaries of Karbala, at the age of 8. He studied under some of Karbala's most senior scholars

In 1967, under guidance of Ayatollah Muhammad as-Shirazi, al-Modarresi established a religious activist group, known as the Risali Movement (الحركة الرسالية), meaning those who follow and deliver the divine message of Islam.

Before the Iranian revolution, the group remained a secret organisation, working on raising religious awareness, however, after the revolution, in 1979, it went public, calling for Islamic movements in the region, with different aliases across various countries.

In Iraq, it was known as the Islamic Action Organisation; in occupied Arabia, it was known as the Islamic Revolution of the Arabian Peninsula; in Bahrain, it was known as the Islamic Front for the Liberation of Bahrain, headed by his brother Ayatollah Syed Hadi al-Modarresi.

During this period, Ayatollah al-Modarresi also focused on producing a methodology that reflected the evolution of the Tafkiki movement, those who seek to decouple Twelver Shi'i scholastic methodology from what it considers to be resources alien to puritanical Islam; those sciences led by Aristotelian and Sufi philosophies and to re-favour knowledge as presented by the Shi'i Imams. In doing so Ayatollah al-Modarresi produced works such as the epistemological work, *Fikr al-Islami*, the philosophical work, *'Irfan al-Islami*, the activists guidelines, *Fi Suluk al-Risali*, the several volume demonstrative jurisprudential work *Tashree' al-Islami*, and the twelve volume Qur'anic exegesis, *Min Huda al-Qur'an*.

It was during the last years of the life of his mentor Ayatollah Mohammed as-Shirazi that Ayatollah al-Modarresi declared his *marja'iyyah* as an example of a supreme religious authority.

Due to the rising pressures of Saddam al-Hussain's Ba'thist government, Ayatollah al-Modarresi emigrated to Kuwait in 1971. He settled there until 1979, after which he moved to Iran after the Islamic Revolution and fought on the battlefields against the Ba'thist led war.

Immediately after the overthrow of Saddam, Ayatollah al-Modarresi returned to Iraq to re-establish the Islamic Seminary *(Hawzah)* and *marja'iyyah* in Kerbala. On his return to Iraq on 22 April 2003, Ayatollah al-Modarresi was arrested along with his entourage by US military personnel. During the following tumultuous period, assasination attempts were made upon his life. This did not distract Ayatollah al-Modarresi from his mission, even resorting to hiding in the trunk of his car to ensure he reached the Seminary where he would continue conducting his classes.

The Islamic Action Organization became an Iraqi Shia Islamist political party with al-Modaressi as its leader. The party contested subsequent elections. Ayatollah al-Modarresi was the first Shia religious leader to issue a call to popular resistance against ISIS, following a dream in which he saw the funeral procession of Imam 'Ali ﷺ being attacked, interpreting it as the outcome if he and the religious authorities did not immediately act.

In December 2014, Ayatollah al-Modarresi was invited by the Pope to attend a summit of world religious leaders at the Vatican. This made him the first Grand Ayatollah to have met the Pope. In 2016 he went to Australia where he met community leaders as well as the Australian Foreign Minister Julie Bishop. In 2020 he partook in a conference organised by the Prime Minister of Iceland on the religious responses to global warming.

Ayatollah al-Modarresi is known as a leading thinker, jurist and author of more than 400 books. His methodology is rooted in the Qur'an, rationality and political awareness, evidenced by his daily exegetical classes, weekly political review and various international TV channels. Amongst his recent works includes *Hayaatun Tayyibah*, a novel juristic work on how to live a pure life across the many spheres of daily life.

His office can be found on social media including Twitter and Instagram.

Personal Notes

Chapter One

Sanctity of the Self

Life is amongst the foundational rights for the human being. It is a value of faith stemming from the respect for others and the recognition of all their rights. Thus, the sanctity of the soul is one the most profound sanctities mentioned in the Qur'an.

Peace is a noble goal for the Islamic community, and providing a prosperous livelihood is among its most prominent pillars which depends on food, drink, housing, health and education.

Because food has been made a primary need for the human being, therefore feeding people is a primary responsibility, and all food is made permissible to the human except what Allah ﷻ has prohibited (which in reality is but a few).

It is upon the person to look into the matters of his nourishment and choose what is purest from it for food produces the energy that must be spent in piety and benevolence. So, it is upon the person to protect the sanctity of his food intake.

Food and its Relationship to the Value of Life as Mentioned in the Holy Qur'an

﴿وَإِذَا قِيلَ لَهُمْ أَنفِقُوا مِمَّا رَزَقَكُمُ اللَّهُ قَالَ الَّذِينَ كَفَرُوا

لِلَّذِينَ ءَامَنُوا أَنُطْعِمُ مَن لَوْ يَشَآءُ اللَّهُ أَطْعَمَهُ إِنْ أَنتُمْ إِلاَّ فِي
ضَلاَلٍ مُبِينٍ ﴿٤٧﴾

1. And when they are told: 'Give to others out of what God has provided for you,' the disbelievers say to the believers: 'Why should we feed those that God could feed if He wanted? You must be deeply misguided.' (33:47)

﴿وَلَمْ نَكُ نُطْعِمُ الْمِسْكِينَ ﴿٤٤﴾﴾

2. And we did not feed the poor. (74:44)

﴿أَوْ إِطْعَامٌ فِي يَوْمٍ ذِي مَسْغَبَةٍ ﴿١٤﴾﴾

3. Or to feed at a time of hunger. (90:14)

﴿إِنَّهُ كَانَ لاَ يُؤْمِنُ بِاللَّهِ الْعَظِيمِ ﴿٣٣﴾ وَلاَ يَحُضُّ عَلَى طَعَامِ
الْمِسْكِينِ ﴿٣٤﴾﴾

4. He would not believe in Almighty God; And he never encouraged feeding the hungry. (69:33-34)

﴿وَلاَ تَحَاضُّونَ عَلَى طَعَامِ الْمِسْكِينِ ﴿١٨﴾﴾

5. You do not urge one another to feed the poor. (89:18)

﴿قَالَ تَزْرَعُونَ سَبْعَ سِنِينَ دَأَباً فَمَا حَصَدتُّم فَذَرُوهُ فِي سُنْبُلِهِ
إِلاَّ قَلِيلاً مِمَّا تَأْكُلُونَ ﴿٤٧﴾﴾

6. Then I can return to the people to inform them.' He (Joseph)

said: 'You will sow for seven consecutive years as usual. Store all that you reap, left in the ear, apart from the little you eat. (12:47)

﴿هُوَ الَّذِى جَعَلَ لَكُمُ الأَرْضَ ذَلُولاً فَامْشُوا فِى مَنَاكِبِهَا وَكُلُوا
مِن رِزْقِهِ وَإِلَيْهِ النُّشُورُ ﴿١٥﴾﴾

7. It is He who has made the earth manageable for you - travel its regions; eat His provision, and to Him you will be resurrected. (67:15)

﴿إِنَّمَا تَعْبُدُونَ مِن دُونِ اللَّهِ أَوْثَاناً وَتَخْلُقُونَ إِفْكاً إِنَّ الَّذِينَ
تَعْبُدُونَ مِن دُونِ اللَّهِ لاَ يَمْلِكُونَ لَكُمْ رِزْقاً فَابْتَغُوا عِندَ
اللَّهِ الرِّزْقَ وَاعْبُدُوهُ وَاشْكُرُوا لَهُ إِلَيْهِ تُرْجَعُونَ ﴿١٧﴾﴾

8. What you worship instead of God are mere idols; what you invent is nothing but falsehood. Those you serve instead of God have no power to give you provisions, so seek provisions from God, serve Him, and give Him thanks: you will all be returned to Him. (29:17)

﴿وَكُلُوا مِمَّا رَزَقَكُمُ اللَّهُ حَلاَلاً طَيِّباً وَاتَّقُوا اللَّهَ الَّذِى أَنْتُمْ بِهِ
مُؤْمِنُونَ ﴿٨٨﴾﴾

9. And eat the lawful and good things that God provides for you. Be mindful of God, in whom you believe. (5:88)

﴿لِيُنفِقْ ذُو سَعَةٍ مِن سَعَتِهِ وَمَن قُدِرَ عَلَيْهِ رِزْقُهُ فَلْيُنفِقْ مِمَّآ

ءَاتَـاهُ اللَّهُ لاَ يُكَلِّفُ اللَّهُ نَفْسـاً إِلاَّ مَـآ ءَاتَاهَـا سَـيَجْعَلُ اللَّهُ
بَعْـدَ عُسْرٍ يُـسْرًا ﴿٧﴾

10. And let the wealthy person spend according to his wealth. But let him whose provision is restricted spend according to what God has given him: God does not burden any soul with more than He has given it after hardship, God will bring ease. (65:7)

Food and its Relationship to the Value of Life as Mentioned in the Noble Sunnah

1. The Messenger of Allah Mohammed ﷺ said: “He did not truly believe in me the one who sleeps satiated and his neighbour is hungry.” In addition, he has also said: “On the Day of Judgement, Allah would not not look (mercifully) at the people of a town whilst among them is someone who sleeps hungry.”[1]

2. Ameer al-Mo’mineen Ali ibn Abi Talib ؑ is narrated to have said: “The believer is not to be satiated whilst his brother is hungry.”[2]

3. Imam Ja’far as-Sadiq ؑ is narrated to have said: “Whoever is compelled to eat the animal that has died without slaughter or consume from its blood or the meat of a pig but chooses not to eat any of it such until he dies of starvation, he dies an ingrate and rejector.”[3]

Food and its Relationship to the Value of Life and Insights Extrapolated from the Divine Sources

Food is a Primary Need for All

Food is the primary need of mankind such that searching for it, acquiring it, and consuming it is a duty just as feeding those unable to do so is a religious and moral duty of people. This is a duty to preserve and save it (food) for the day it is needed is important.

Allah ﷻ has also commanded to strive for ones sustenance, and the noble verses of the Qur'an indicate toward the necessity of eating and drinking by virtue of the language evidencing the need to preserve one's life just as rationality guides us toward that too. The religious texts also evidence the obligation of feeding the needy and destitute and spending out of what Allah ﷻ has provided.

Food and its Relationship to the Value of Life and Details of the Rulings

1. It is religiously incumbent upon a person to strive in earning a living and not to place its burden on others. Hence it is prohibited to restrain or holdback (oneself) from earning if he is capable of working and earning a livelihood by lawful and conventional means.

2. Also, it is obligatory to eat and drink to the amount that preserves life from damage, or severe injuries such as illness or excessive weakness.

3. If the severely hungry person finds nothing but prohibited foods or drink, he must eat and drink from it to what preserves him from

death.

4. It is preferable to eat from the purer and healthier foods without specifying one kind or the other, for Allah ﷻ has made in every source and sustenance of livelihood a benefit and pleasure.

5. It is preferable to eat the fruits when ripened.

6. It is upon a person not to use his energy generated from eating as a means of sowing corruption and following the footstep of Satan but rather to thank his Lord (for the food) and act righteously.

7. He must take into consideration the limits of eating and drinking, so that he does not waste or have excess nor does he eat the illgotten or prohibited and so on.

8. A person must give due rights to food by spending appropriately according to the following points:

a. Everyone should base their personal finances on the basis of keeping the rights of the poor and destitute; that is that he should avoid overspending on his personal expenses especially when it comes to matters of luxury and entertainment so that [that money can instead] be spread to those in need. Perhaps the bread crumbs [little amount] that gathers on the tables of a rich country is sufficient to feed a poor nation poor in their entirety. And what the rich lavish on smoking and appetisers, the variety of drinks and decorating of houses and regularly changing cars without such needs, may be sufficient to recruit every unemployed hand in their countries. Indeed truthful was the Commander of the Faithful, Imam Ali ﷺ who said: "I have not seen any abundant blessing except with a squandered squandered right by its side."[4]

b. Upon each individual is to enquire about (be aware of the situation of) his neighbours, relatives and people of his country (area) so that there would be (remain) no hungry destitute person amongst them, and if he were to find anyone in that situation he would satiate him.

c. Upon the state is to organise and regulate their economic rules in a way that prevents deprivation, poverty and destitution, narrowing the gap between classes and increasing social solidarity because the human family is one and there exists in the world places that are deprived and devastated, there is need of food aid. It is necessary all people are interested in this (providing aid) and organise their assistance in various ways. It is not sufficient, the existing humanitarian organisations (such as the Red Cross or the International Red Crescent), because their presence until now has not fulfilled the growing need for aid.

d. The Muslim world must strive hard in the way of achieving food security because food is of the primary necessities of life and its neglect is considered a threat to life, security and the independence of people.

Commentary: A Holistic Approach to Food

Eating is not just about how physically appealing the food is, how tasty it is or how many calories it contains. Food is medicine for the body, it is unique coding and information for the different processes that are required for us to function optimally. The food we consume is not only important for the purposes of digestion and the gut but influences every system in a complex manner that has kept scientists researching for many years.

It is fascinating that simple activities of daily living such as movement or breathing, can only be achieved by intricate biochemical reactions that adjust and rebalance on a regular basis to keep our bodies alive, independent and healthy.

As an example, let's look at mitochondria, a organelle in our body also known as the power-house of energy. Its intricate design (figure 1) and structure provides the best environment for producing and releasing energy for us. For the outer structure of the cell to stay in good condition we are in need of key healthy fats (2) (3) (4) (5) (6).

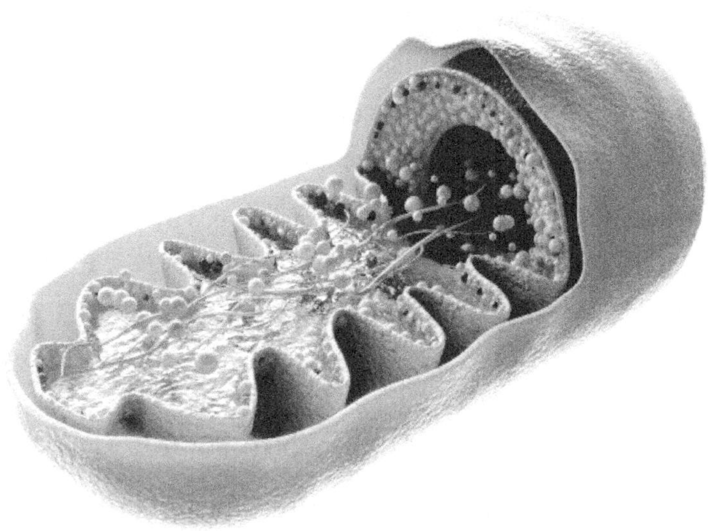

Figure 1

Within the mitochondria, a complex cycle of energy production is carried out. Each part of the cycle requires specific nutrients such as zinc, iron, magnesium and B vitamins.

In addition to the process of production of energy, known as ATP, we also need to be able transport ATP from within the mitochondria out into our blood stream.

This transportation mechanism requires a variety of essential proteins.

This example shows the importance of consuming a nutrient dense diet that includes a variety of fruits and vegetables, proteins and healthy fats.

Food is code for our body to carry out the right chemical pathways that we need to function. Nutrient depleted foods such as processed foods do not give us the right coding, in fact they can change the coding to form negative outcomes.

The relationship between food and energy is common knowledge, by understanding the detail pathways that are required, it allows us to appreciate the interconnections of what we eat with how we utilize energy for daily activities. There are other relationships of food to our body that are not so commonly discussed. As an example, the relationship between our mental state and food (7) (8) (9) (10) (11) (12).

We discard this relationship in our daily life, but it is not foreign to us. We experience the reaction of food on our mental state on a regular basis, for example many of us will notice after a big lunch loaded with processed cheese and bread (i.e. a pizza or a sandwich), the feeling of the 'post lunch brain fog' making us sleepy and lack focus; or giving their child ice cream just before bed only to have to deal with their hyperactivity afterwards.

These seem to be short lived and so we do not pay much attention to them. But a buildup of a poor diet, lacking in nutrients, can have profound impact on long term focus, attention and memory (8).

In one particular study on rats, it evidences that a poor maternal diet may have generational impact, a whole two or three generations down their lineage seem to be impacted with lack of attention, focus and brain fog! (13) (14).

These examples are only touching the surface of how significantly our choice of the type of food we consume can affect our bodies daily function. But it is not only the type of food, some believe that how we grow our food, who grows our food and what the plant or animal has been through can dictate how our bodies perceive it, friend or foe.

The most common experiment being Dr. Masaru Emoto's work, *The Hidden Messengers in Water*, whereby Dr. Emoto discovered a change in crystal formation depending on the type of words shared with water (15). Positive words had significant impact on the type and beauty of the crystals that formed. Just imagine the impact we could be having on the food we consume, since water is essential to life and exists in all living creatures, we are more than 70% water and eat plants containing water.

Dr. Emoto's work reminds us of a verse in the Holy Qur'an relating to the words we speak:

﴿أَلَمْ تَرَ كَيْفَ ضَرَبَ اللَّهُ مَثَلًا كَلِمَةً طَيِّبَةً كَشَجَرَةٍ طَيِّبَةٍ أَصْلُهَا ثَابِتٌ وَفَرْعُهَا فِي السَّمَاءِ ﴿٢٤﴾﴾

Have you not considered how Allah presents an example, [making] a good word like a good tree, whose root is firmly fixed and its branches [high] in the sky? (14:24)

﴿تُؤْتِي أُكُلَهَا كُلَّ حِينٍ بِإِذْنِ رَبِّهَا ۗ وَيَضْرِبُ اللَّهُ الْأَمْثَالَ لِلنَّاسِ لَعَلَّهُمْ يَتَذَكَّرُونَ ﴿٢٥﴾﴾

It produces its fruit all the time, by permission of its Lord. And Allah presents examples for the people that perhaps they will be reminded. (14:25)

﴿وَمَثَلُ كَلِمَةٍ خَبِيثَةٍ كَشَجَرَةٍ خَبِيثَةٍ اجْتُثَّتْ مِنْ فَوْقِ الْأَرْضِ مَا لَهَا مِنْ قَرَارٍ ﴿٢٦﴾﴾

And the example of a bad word is like a bad tree, uprooted from the surface of the earth, not having any stability. (14:26)

Journalists Glenn Greenwald and Leighton Woodhouse have authored a most stunning article arguing factory farming is one of the most revolting byproducts of modern industrial society, where principles of the "free market" are used to justify torture-derived products being available to consumers like "nearly 280 million laying hens confined in barren wire battery cages so restrictive the birds can't even spread their wings."

And what are their conditions exactly like? The article quotes a worker in such farms who states: 'Cages were about the size of a microwave, with seven to ten hens crammed into each one. The floors were made of an abrasive wire mesh, so when birds died – often from thirst or starvation after their confinement had debilitated their muscles and bones, rendering them paralysed – the live hens would stand on top of the decaying carcasses to give their feet some relief.'[5]

Truly, people can only stomach their food when they are kept ignorant of where it actually came from!

It begs us to ask the question: Could our practices of spiritual, metaphysical nature that are having profound physical impacts on plants and animals also influence our human nature and character when we consume them?

If a food is grown or left in an environment of negative communication or negative energy, such as cruelty to animals or produced from slave labour, it may transfer this negativity to us. Are these not then influencing the souls? Is it not "the example of a bad word is like a bad tree"?

In relation to Ayatollah al-Modarressi's work that discusses some of the nature of the human being's greed and the need to support those who are destitute, he states a profound example of how we act as humans: "Perhaps the bread crumbs [little amount] that gathers on the tables of a rich country is sufficient to feed a poor nation poor in their entirety. And what the rich lavish on smoking and appetisers, the variety of drinks and decorating of houses and regularly changing cars without such needs, may be sufficient to recruit every unemployed hand in their countries."

I pose an additional question: Could the soul of the person in charge of preparation, growth and ultimately selling of food, have an impact on the physical properties of the food we eat? What if the characteristic of greed resides in their heart and affects the atomic content of the food we consume? Once we consume such food could it be affecting the nature of our souls creating a viscous cycle that keeps feeding the characteristic of greed in mankind, similar to the study of the generational impact of diet on rats.

In contrast, is it possible that eating a meal with others in an act of selflessness, positively affects chemical reactions inside the human body and beautifies the soul with the characteristic of generosity?

Scientists have already been looking into the effects of eating alone versus with others. They have noted that eating alone may increase the likelihood of obesity and metabolic syndrome (15). Whereas eating with others helps to increase positivity which boosts the immune system and creates a better digestive process, in addition to laughter and a relaxed mindset.

Of course, this may be assuming that the person you are eating with is one who has a good soul. However, the discussion brings together the possibility that what we consume, how we consume it and who we consume it with can have a profound impact on the soul of a human being.

It urges us to rethink our meal times, to rethink what we buy in a supermarket and what we advertise to our children.

Throughout the book, we have provided some reflection activity sections, the first of which is presented below.

Nutrition

CODING FOR THE BODY

Communication
bringing balance to the body

Information
coding system

Energy
protecting your powerhouse

Medicine
healing properties

What's in your '*pizza*' of nutrition?

Endnotes

1 The Arabic text states:

قال رسول الله صلى الله عليه وآله: ما آمن بي من بات شبعان وجاره جائع وقال: ما من أهل قرية يبيت فيهم جائع ينظر الله إليهم يوم القيامة

2 The Arabic text states:

وروي عن الإمام أمير المؤمنين عليه السلام قوله: لا يشبع المؤمن وأخوه جائع

3 The Arabic text states:

قال الإمام الصادق عليه السلام: من اضطر إلى الميتة والدم ولحم الخنزير فلم يأكل شيئاً من ذلك حتى يموت فهو كافر.

4 The Arabic text states:

قال علي عليه السلام: ما رأيت نعمة موفورة إلا وبجانبها حق مضيَّع

5 www.theintercept.com/2018/03/02/consumers-are-revolting-against-animal-cruelty-so-the-poultry-industry-is-lobbying-for-laws-to-force-stores-to-sell-their-eggs/

Personal Notes

Chapter Two

Principle of Permissibility of Food

What is Mentioned in the Holy Qur'an

﴿الْيَوْمَ أُحِلَّ لَكُمُ الطَّيِّبَاتُ وَطَعَامُ الَّذِينَ أُوتُوا الْكِتَابَ حِلٌّ لَكُمْ وَطَعَامُكُمْ حِلٌّ لَهُمْ...﴿٥﴾﴾

This day [all] good foods have been made lawful, and the food of those who were given the Scripture is lawful for you and your food is lawful for them. (5:5)

﴿قُلْ لَا أَجِدُ فِي مَا أُوحِيَ إِلَيَّ مُحَرَّماً عَلَى طَاعِمٍ يَطْعَمُهُ إِلَّا أَنْ يَكُونَ مَيْتَةً أَوْ دَماً مَسْفُوحاً أَوْ لَحْمَ خِنْزِيرٍ فَإِنَّهُ رِجْسٌ أَوْ فِسْقاً أُهِلَّ لِغَيْرِ اللهِ بِهِ فَمَنِ اضْطُرَّ غَيْرَ بَاغٍ وَلَا عَادٍ فَإِنَّ رَبَّكَ غَفُورٌ رَحِيمٌ﴿١٤٥﴾﴾

Say: "I do not find within that which was revealed to me [anything] forbidden to one who would eat it unless it be a dead animal or blood spilled out or the flesh of swine - for indeed, it is impure - or it be [that slaughtered in] disobedience, dedicated to other than Allah. But whoever is forced [by necessity], neither desiring [it] nor transgressing [its limit], then indeed, your Lord is Forgiving and Merciful. (6:145)

﴿أُحِلَّ لَكُمْ صَيْدُ الْبَحْرِ وَطَعَامُهُ مَتَاعاً لَكُمْ وَلِلسَّيَّارَةِ
وَحُرِّمَ عَلَيْكُمْ صَيْدُ الْبَرِّ مَا دُمْتُمْ حُرُماً وَاتَّقُوا اللَّهَ الَّذِي
إِلَيْهِ تُحْشَرُونَ ﴿٩٦﴾﴾

Lawful to you is game from the sea and its food as provision for you and the travelers, but forbidden to you is game from the land as long as you are in the state of ihram. And fear Allah to whom you will be gathered. (5:96)

﴿كُلُّ الطَّعَامِ كَانَ حِلاًّ لِبَنِي إِسْرَآئِيلَ إِلاَّ مَا حَرَّمَ إِسْرَآئِيلُ
عَلَى نَفْسِهِ مِن قَبْلِ أَن تُنَزَّلَ التَّوْرَاةُ قُلْ فَأْتُواْ بِالتَّوْرَاةِ
فَاتْلُوهَآ إِن كُنْتُمْ صَادِقِينَ ﴿٩٣﴾﴾

All food was lawful to the Children of Israel except what Israel had made unlawful to himself before the Torah was revealed. Say [O Muhammad]: "So bring the Torah and recite it, if you should be truthful." (3:93)

﴿وَقَالُوا هَٰذِهِ أَنْعَامٌ وَحَرْثٌ حِجْرٌ لاَ يَطْعَمُهَا إِلاَّ مَن نَشَآءُ

بِزَعْمِهِمْ وَأَنْعَامٌ حُرِّمَتْ ظُهُورُهَا وَأَنْعَامٌ لَا يَذْكُرُونَ اسْمَ
اللَّهِ عَلَيْهَا افْتِرَاءً عَلَيْهِ سَيَجْزِيهِم بِمَا كَانُوا يَفْتَرُونَ ﴿١٣٨﴾

And they say: "These animals and crops are forbidden; no one may eat from them except whom we will," by their claim. And there are those [camels] whose backs are forbidden [by them] and those upon which the name of Allah is not mentioned - [all of this] an invention of untruth about Him. He will punish them for what they were inventing. (6:138)

What is Mentioned in the Noble Sunnah

1. Mohammed bin Muslim and Zurarah bin A'yun both asked Imam al-Baqir about the permissibility of eating the meat of a domesticated donkey and he replied: "The Messenger of Allah prohibited eating it on the day of the Battle of Khaybar. Rather he (temporarily) prohibited eating it at that time only because it was a means of transport for people. However, what is (permanently) prohibited is what is mentioned as prohibited in the Qur'an."[1]

2. Imam Ja'far as-Sadiq said: "My father (Imam al-Baqir) was asked about eating the meat of the domesticated donkey. He replied: 'The Messenger of Allah prohibited its eating because during that time it was a means of transport for people. What is (permanently) prohibited is what Allah mentioned as prohibited in the Qur'an.'"[2]

Insights Extrapolated from the Divine Sources

Islam is a legislation of tolerance and laws are easy and not difficult to follow by which Allah has removed the shackles from the mind of mankind and the burdens which people shoulder. He restored to them the freedoms that He created them upon. And one of it's dimensions (general principle of legislative tolerance) is the permissibility of matters until known otherwise by a certainty yielding source and the ritual purity of things until made impure by a clear evidence. Thus, the principle of the permissibility of food consumption which Allah ﷻ has provided for us, is the case until there is a clear text to say otherwise. This is a very useful principle, indeed.

Details of the Rulings

We benefit from the verses of the Holy Qur'an which we mentioned by a number of general provisions:

1. Allah ﷻ has allowed mankind to benefit from whatever is on the earth, and it is not permissible for people to prohibit or deny it to themselves or to each other, which would limit a person's progress and activity.

2. All good livelihoods are *halaal* and the religion has not prohibited except what is specified and indicated by the particular texts.

3. Allah ﷻ has not prohibited of food except what the noble verses of the Quran have clearly mentioned; other than those it is considered permissible and good. If it is stated in the *hadith* that some food is prohibited, it would be prohibited in the sense of what seeks to keep you purified and away from something that would foul the soul and not forbidden in the sense of legislation. In other words, it is dis-recommended but not outright prohibited.[3]

This third insight differs amongst scholars, however, here are the details of these three insights:

First: Utilising what is in the Earth, as per the Holy Qur'an

﴿الَّذِى جَعَلَ لَكُمُ الأَرْضَ مَهْداً وَسَلَكَ لَكُمْ فِيهَا سُبُلاً وَأَنزَلَ مِنَ السَّمَآءِ مَآءً فَأَخْرَجْنَا بِهِ أَزْوَاجاً مِن نَبَاتٍ شَتَّى ﴿٥٣﴾﴾

He it is Who made the earth for you an expanse and made for you therein paths and sent down water from the cloud; then thereby We have brought forth many species of various herbs. (20:53)

﴿الَّذِى جَعَلَ لَكُم مِنَ الشَّجَرِ الأَخْضَرِ نَاراً فَإِذَآ أَنتُم مِنْهُ تُوقِدُونَ ﴿٨٠﴾﴾

He Who has made for you the fire (to burn) from the green tree, so that with it you kindle (fire). (36:80)

﴿هُوَ الَّذِى جَعَلَ لَكُمُ الأَرْضَ ذَلُولاً فَامْشُوا فِى مَنَاكِبِهَا وَكُلُوا مِن رِزْقِهِ وَإِلَيْهِ النُّشُورُ ﴿١٥﴾﴾

He it is Who made the earth smooth for you, therefore go about in the spacious sides thereof, and eat of His sustenance, and to Him is the return after death. (67:15)

﴿وَكُلُوا مِمَّا رَزَقَكُمُ اللهُ حَلَالاً طَيِّباً وَاتَّقُوا اللهَ الَّذِى أَنْتُمْ بِهِ مُؤْمِنُونَ ﴿٨٨﴾﴾

> And eat of the lawful and good (things) that Allah has given you, and be careful of (your duty to) Allah, in Whom you believe. (5:88)

Utilising what is in the Earth, as per the Noble Sunnah

1. Mohammed bin Sinan narrated from Abi al-Hasan Ali al-Hadi ﷺ who asked him ﷺ about the water of a valley who replied: "Verily Muslims are equal stakeholders and partners in water, fire and pasture."[4]

2. Imam Ali ﷺ is narrated to have said: "It is not permitted to prevent (the usage) of salt or water."[5]

Insights Extrapolated from the Divine Sources

Everyone has the right to benefit from the earth which Allah ﷻ has paved for people and follow the paths He ﷻ eased (of natural resources) for them without distinction (for their availability and usage) between humans and another.

In addition, every human has the right (freedom) to benefit from what is deep within the earth, from its paths thereof and from the sustenance of Allah ﷻ therein, just as the energy generated by fire is the property of all.

Details of the Rulings

1. No State, nation, denomination or person is permitted to prevent people from utilising what is in the earth of agricultural areas, running water, pastures or visible or hidden minerals.

2. All people may derive and extract the benefits of the land they wish provided that they do not deprive others of them, because

they are not for them especially, but for everyone.

3. Society may establish laws to regulate the use of natural resources provided that no ones right shall be lost on behalf of the other as per the extent of what is necessary, because the fundamental freedoms of human beings may only be violated or prejudiced to the extent necessary.

4. It is not permissible to block or close roads (or any accesses) from the movement of people in the earth except for a vital need whether that movement was for economic purposes (such as trade or agricultural and industrial investment) or for tourism, guidance or learning.

Commentary: What we Eat

Our discussions have been pertaining to areas of food that impact the quality, sustenance and nourishment of what we consume. Before even putting a morsel of food into our mouth, we are drawn to pause, reflect and thank. Of course, what we then choose to consume will undoubtedly have impact on our physical bodies.

Some of the latest research in the field of medicine has discussed the major role of gut health on disease. One fantastic paper released in the year 2020, titled: *All disease, begins in the (leaky) gut* by A. Fasano'' (37). Fasano is a world-renowned researcher covering numerous topics related to gut permeability and the leaky gut.

It is important to note that in Prophetic traditions the gut was also discussed as the root of disease.

In fact, we have a narration from Imam Musa al-Kadhim ﷺ that states: "Diet control is the fountain-head of remedies and the stomach is the house of all ailments, so condition your body while it can be conditioned."[6] (38)

Discussion Point
Have we neglected the power of the gut in our health? What shall habit changes can we make to honour the blessings of our gut?

There are two key aspects of the gut that assist with preventing disease. If these two are dysfunctional then disease is imminent.

The first is the gut wall.

Your intestines are the size of a tennis court and for good reason. Usually your gut wall is like a mesh or a cheese cloth. It consists of small tiny holes and does not allow big foreign objects to penetrate inside of your body. In order for large foreign objects such as proteins to seep through this wall, enzymes are produced to cut them into small tiny pieces. Your long intestines give more time for the body to break these large proteins down and help your body digest and assimilate.

However, if this wall has had damage due to poor diet (excessive inflammation), lack of exercise (effects tissue tone and blood flow) and stress (excessive inflammation and poor neurotransmission) then the small holes of the gut turn in to large gaps. This allows large molecules to pass through the gut wall. The body is not used to this, so it creates an in-flammatory response. This is positive as it helps to protect you, but only if it happens a couple of times. If the process happens repeatedly then you enter a state of chronic inflammation. This is not positive. Chronic inflammation can cause a cascade of issues that can affect organs and other tissues of the body, not to mention that a leaky gut can also allow bacteria and viruses to penetrate unnoticed into the body. Dr. Fasano lays out several chronic diseases such as autoimmune conditions, cancers, mental health disorders and neuroinflammatory diseases which begin due to the phenomena of a 'leaky gut'.

Are we now getting a clearer understanding of the Prophetic traditions relating gut health to disease?

The second is your gut microbiome. The microbiome of your gut is like a rainforest. It holds many different species of bacteria. Yes, that is correct, bacteria! In fact, your body is more microbes (such as bacteria, fungi and viruses) than it is human. Research has now found that these microbes are so important that they could be the main treatment for lots of health conditions (39). Ideally you should have a broad variety of these microbes as each one feeds on prebiotics from food we eat, such as onions, garlic, leeks and asparagus. After feasting on this delicious food, they produce different metabolites.

One really important by-product is butyrate. This short chain fatty acid is phenomenal. It is known to help keep the body in balance (homeostasis) by reducing inflammation and preventing cancer (40) (41). It also prevents you from having a leaky gut by assisting the growth of the hair like projections on your gut lining, called villi.

Remember, a healthy gut lining also stops other toxins from entering your body. This is why it is so important to eat a variety of different fruits and vegetables to maintain this rainforest of good bacteria that live in your gut.

This may be why Allah ﷻ links eating of pure and good things to your giving thanks for your health and wellbeing:

﴿وَاذْكُرُوا إِذْ أَنتُمْ قَلِيلٌ مُّسْتَضْعَفُونَ فِي الْأَرْضِ تَخَافُونَ أَن يَتَخَطَّفَكُمُ النَّاسُ فَآوَاكُمْ وَأَيَّدَكُم بِنَصْرِهِ وَرَزَقَكُم مِّنَ الطَّيِّبَاتِ لَعَلَّكُمْ تَشْكُرُونَ ﴿٢٦﴾﴾

> And remember the time when you were few [and] helpless on earth, fearful lest people do away with you whereupon He sheltered you, and strengthened you with His succour, and provided for you sustenance out of the good things of life, so that you might have cause to be grateful. (8:26)

Another important chemical produced by the gut bacteria is called serotonin. You may have heard of this as the 'happiness molecule'. It is known to contribute to wellbeing and happiness. It is commonly thought that serotonin is only a brain derived chemical, however, in actual fact, over 75% of the serotonin is produced in the gut (42).

Scientists managed to stumble across this after giving antidepressants, that are known to keep serotonin floating in the blood stream for longer, to patients who also had irritable bowel syndrome. These patients responded well and it prompted research into the reasons.

Serotonin is extremely important for bowel motions, appetite and to prevent you eating something toxic. It helps to increase the transit time of toxic food that you don't want to be having in your system, so you can get rid of it! Not to mention, it has major effects on mood, anxiety and overall wellbeing.

Once again, this further emphasises the need for eating the good healthy foods and a variety of different colours of foods to support these creatures living in your gut lining. Is Allah ﷻ guiding us towards this idea in the verse:

﴿الَّذِي جَعَلَ لَكُمُ الْأَرْضَ مَهْدًا وَسَلَكَ لَكُمْ فِيهَا سُبُلًا وَأَنزَلَ مِنَ السَّمَاءِ مَاءً فَأَخْرَجْنَا بِهِ أَزْوَاجًا مِّن نَّبَاتٍ شَتَّىٰ ﴿٥٣﴾﴾

He it is Who made the earth for you an expanse and made for you therein paths and sent down water from the cloud; then thereby We have brought forth many species of various herbs. (20:53)

﴿وَمَا ذَرَأَ لَكُمْ فِي الْأَرْضِ مُخْتَلِفًا أَلْوَانُهُ ۗ إِنَّ فِي ذَٰلِكَ لَآيَةً لِّقَوْمٍ يَذَّكَّرُونَ ﴿١٣﴾﴾

And [He has subjected] whatever He multiplied for you on the earth of varying colors. Indeed in that is a sign for a people who remember. (16:13)

Practical Tips

1. Healing the gut wall: The first step is to remove damaging foods. Start with simple steps:

- Avoid general unhealthy options such as refined sugars, highly processed food and meat, processed fats and oils.

Quick tip: A highly processed food can be categorized as a packaged product having more than 5 ingredients.

- You may have genetic susceptibility to certain foods, most commonly wheat and dairy. This would require further investigations, but you could try eliminating them for a period of three weeks and adding them back one by one, observing how your body reacts.

- The gut wall can also be irritated and inflamed by toxic relationships, lack of movement and stress. Mend your friendships with love, go for a walk and supplicate to improve trust in God.

Practical Tips Continued

- There has been evidence to suggest specific foods may help the lining of the gut, such as bone broth (2), oil of oregano (3), antioxidants and Omega-3 fish oils (4).

2. Feeding the gut microbiome – the 'rainforest' of good bacteria are fed by eating a variety of different foods.

Quick Tip: Think about all the colours of the rainbow and try to add these different colour fruits and vegetables into your diet. We should really be aiming for seven different types each day. Adding all these wonderful herbs, spices and fermented foods helps diversify the gut microbiome.

Second: Goodly and Permissible God-Given Sustenance, as per the Holy Qur'an

﴿يَـٰٓأَيُّهَا ٱلَّذِينَ ءَامَنُوا۟ كُلُوا۟ مِن طَيِّبَـٰتِ مَا رَزَقْنَـٰكُمْ
وَٱشْكُرُوا۟ لِلَّهِ إِن كُنتُمْ إِيَّاهُ تَعْبُدُونَ ﴿١٧٢﴾﴾

O you who have believed, eat from the good things which We have provided for you and be grateful to Allah if it is [indeed] Him that you worship. (2:172)

﴿ٱلَّذِينَ يَتَّبِعُونَ ٱلرَّسُولَ ٱلنَّبِىَّ ٱلْأُمِّىَّ ٱلَّذِى يَجِدُونَهُۥ مَكْتُوبًا
عِندَهُمْ فِى ٱلتَّوْرَىٰةِ وَٱلْإِنجِيلِ يَأْمُرُهُم بِٱلْمَعْرُوفِ وَيَنْهَىٰهُمْ
عَنِ ٱلْمُنكَرِ وَيُحِلُّ لَهُمُ ٱلطَّيِّبَـٰتِ وَيُحَرِّمُ عَلَيْهِمُ ٱلْخَبَـٰٓئِثَ
وَيَضَعُ عَنْهُمْ إِصْرَهُمْ وَٱلْأَغْلَـٰلَ ٱلَّتِى كَانَتْ عَلَيْهِمْ فَٱلَّذِينَ
ءَامَنُوا۟ بِهِۦ وَعَزَّرُوهُ وَنَصَرُوهُ وَٱتَّبَعُوا۟ ٱلنُّورَ ٱلَّذِىٓ أُنزِلَ مَعَهُۥٓ
أُو۟لَـٰٓئِكَ هُمُ ٱلْمُفْلِحُونَ ﴿١٥٧﴾﴾

Those who follow the Messenger, the unlettered prophet, whom they find written in what they have of the Torah and the Gospel, who enjoins upon them what is right and forbids them what is wrong and makes lawful for them the good things and prohibits for them the evil and relieves them of their burden and the shackles which were upon them. So they who have believed in him, honoured him, supported him and followed the light which was sent down with him - it is those who will be the successful. (7:157)

﴿يَسْأَلُونَكَ مَاذَا أُحِلَّ لَهُمْ قُلْ أُحِلَّ لَكُمُ الطَّيِّبَاتُ وَمَا عَلَّمْتُم مِّنَ الْجَوَارِحِ مُكَلِّبِينَ تُعَلِّمُونَهُنَّ مِمَّا عَلَّمَكُمُ اللَّهُ فَكُلُوا مِمَّا أَمْسَكْنَ عَلَيْكُمْ وَاذْكُرُوا اسْمَ اللَّهِ عَلَيْهِ وَاتَّقُوا اللَّهَ إِنَّ اللَّهَ سَرِيعُ الْحِسَابِ ﴿٤﴾﴾

They ask you, [O Muhammad], what has been made lawful for them. Say: "Lawful for you are [all] good foods and [game caught by] what you have trained of hunting animals which you train as Allah has taught you. So eat of what they catch for you, and mention the name of Allah upon it, and fear Allah: Indeed, Allah is swift in account." (5:4)

Insights Extrapolated from the Divine Sources

The verses command us to eat from Allah's ﷻ sustenance, what is *halal* and pure, and avoid the impure and soul effecting consumables.

Detail of the Rulings

1. Allah ﷻ has permitted the good and pure things of sustenance only, but as for the impure He has not. But what is the criterion to distinguishing between the pure and distasteful?

2. There are some impure and good things defined by the revelation to humans and others are self-evident and well known to mankind without controversy; people do not vary in them (such as human waste) whilst in others some differ as to what they are:

First: We refer to the revelation for what is defined in the Divine Law as to what is considered adulterating and pure.

Second: We refer to what has been agreed upon by sensible people's standard of general custom and practise.

Third: As part of the above two mentioned points, people of each custom may return to what they considered as good may be eaten and what they found inedible must be avoided.

Commentary: The Balance of the World and its Impact on Food

The world is a gift to us, with its natural beauties and variety, however many of us take this world's bounties for granted. Knowing that there is an afterlife should not give us permission to use the world as we please and we must realize that our life choices have already had an impact in many areas, the most prominent being climate change. There is much evidence relating the human impact on weather pattern changes, oceanic heating and animal extinction (17).

Reflection Point
What can you do to improve your understanding of the source of our food and relationship with nature? How about trying to plant some green herbs in the house?

How does food and our consumption behaviours contribute to this impact? The Qur'an illuminates this point by stating:

﴿وَالسَّمَاءَ رَفَعَهَا وَوَضَعَ الْمِيزَانَ ۝٧﴾

> And the skies has He raised high, and has devised [for all things] a measure. (55:7)

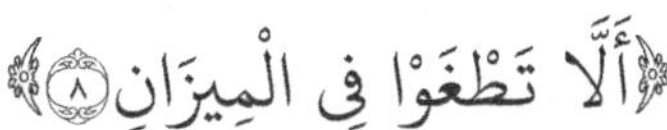

> So that you [too, O humanity,] might never transgress the measure [of what is right]. (55:8)

Allah ﷻ has created our universe in a fine balance. Nature with all its wonder is made with such intricacy and preciseness that one natural herb can have the properties to heal or be poisonousness to the human body.

With the growth of the economy, has come the growth of our stomachs. We have become an on-demand community that has every kind of food at our disposal.

Farming businesses have been driven to meet these demands with new faster and more reliable ways of producing crops, rearing animals and fashioning the best shaped fruit on the supermarket floor. This has led to mass waste of fruits and vegetables that don't 'look normal'.

Reports show that 25% of apples, 20% of onions and 13% of potatoes grown in the UK are wasted on cosmetic grounds.[7]

This may explain why companies like Odd Box, which deliver 'oddly shaped' and 'surplus' fruit and vegetables directly from farms, are becoming more popular.[1]

Our use of pesticides, chemical sprays, unnatural feeding of livestock and many more farming methods are all designed to increase the yield of produce to meet our demands. This has led to a sharp decline in the nutrient density of food and the potential

1 www.oddbox.co.uk

toxic exposure from farming methods to foods that were never known to be toxic (18) (19) (20) (21) (22).

The problem lies in the delayed onset of symptoms that toxic exposure presents with. It is part of the concept of what is known as the exposome. The exposome relates to different environmental factors which can influence your genes and lead to chronic illness (1).

A US based environmental working group tested 10 babies umbilical cord blood and found 200 different industrial chemicals in each new born. This means in a child's first day of life it is already exposed to so many dangerous chemicals.

Over the course of our life we will go on to be exposed to many more different chemicals; to put numbers into perspective, Eurostat, the European Union (EU) statistical office, estimates that the EU produced 81 million tonnes of chemicals hazardous to the environment and 219 million tonnes of chemicals hazardous to human health in 2017 (23).

Surprisingly, we have not learnt from our history.

Research in the area of environmental toxicity is extremely dense and can be accessed by the general public (24; 21).

Media outlets and healthcare facilities have not found it necessary to educate us on these matters. There appears rather, to be a strong push towards medication and their safety and efficacy, but very little towards nutrition and fasting as a means of detoxification or a source of medicine.

Upon reading *Tibb al-Aimma*, a book that has a collection of concepts, supplications and food remedies from the Prophet Muhammad's household ﷺ (25), we have come to the realization that our natural external environment, internal environment and metaphysical realities are extremely interconnected.

Together they are the masters of our overall health.

It is in-built into our nature (fitrah) that medicinal value lies in the natural world God has created for us.

It seems we have distanced ourselves from 'health creation' and have become satisfied with only the immediate 'symptom reliever'. The emphasis on how food can restore balance, food as medicine and the impact of food on chronic health conditions are rarely discussed or shared, but a new drug that we are unsure of its long-term effects will be raised as a saviour of mankind. We are far away from 'health creation' and rather satisfy ourselves with the 'symptom reliever'.

Unfortunately, even with the stringent guidelines faced by scientists, including peer review and randomised control trials, we are plagued with the internal politics, bias, inconsistencies and pay outs to maintain authority (26) (27). It has occurred throughout history and we seem to be following the same pathway.

For example, Roundup is a chemical spray containing glyphosate, it was used on crops in the US in large quantities in order to increase yield and protect them from being eaten by predators. This spray has been classed as a carcinogen (cancer causing substance) by the World Health Organisation due to its effects on the human body. There is history of a big lawsuit case against the company Monsanto that seem to only create the product with profit in mind rather than human health (28).

We have learnt that the breakdown process of the carcinogen found in Roundup takes many years and we till today suffer from the build-up effects in our bodies, which could be the cause of many cancers and diseases (24).

Should we blame these big corporate giants, or are they following our naivety and greed? Arguably, Joel Bakan has provided the clearest answer in his groundbreaking work, *The Corporation: The Pathological Pursuit of Profit and Power*, where he demonstrates the legal requirement of corporations to maximise profit even if it means killing its customers. Truly a must read book.

We are not unintelligent beings that have to follow the dictate of those who are not caring for our well-being other than their own. We have intelligence, we can think for ourselves, we can learn and we have public access to a plethora of material.

Thankfully, there are experts who are waking us up and taking interest in how we are living our lives and its effect on our health. We have entered an era of Integrative Medicine (29). A systems biology approach that understands how our environment, lifestyle and genetics impact our health and the root cause of diseases.

In reality, did we ever leave this era? *Tibb al-Aimma* is bursting with remedies relating to herbs, food and different forms of preparation. (25) It has related the spirit and the mind with how your body heals, through supplications and shifting of a mindset.

The Prophetic life seems to be re-connecting with our current understanding of the nature of healing and health. Although the collection in *Tibb al-Aimma* has specific remedies for certain conditions, we believe these were designed for individual scenarios and symptoms of their time, it is more important that we extract the principles that they taught and practiced.

As an example, a principle dictated by Allah ﷻ in the Holy Quran, is the concept of eating *tayyib*. As Ayatullah al-Modaressi states in Surah al-Baqarah (2), verse 172, Allah ﷻ mentions *halal* alongside *tayyib*. In this particular verse, Allah ﷻ mentions the legislative *halal* alongside the ethical and virtuous *tayyib*. What may be considered *halal* in the legal aspect may not follow guidelines for what is pure, blessed and ethical.

It seems that as a community we have focused our attention on the legislative aspects of religion, but we have taken for granted the ethical, moral and spiritual dimensions of our food, as Imam Khomeini states in the referenced book (30).

We have come across many *"halal"* organisations caught in the media for their inhumane treatment of animals - it may fall within the *halal* but certainly not *tayyib*.

In our current system, we do not question as to the care and love that was provided to an animal before slaughtering. We only question about three major items, was the animal alive, did a Muslim slaughter it, did he say *'bismillah'*. How it was raised and treated appear to be ignored.

Discussion Point

In Surah Al-Hujarat we are provided the example of backbiting being akin to eating the flesh of your brother. It seems to hint towards unethical actions causing metaphysical manifestations and possibly some physical similitudes. Could there also be a relationship between immoral rearing of livestock and the impact this has on our souls?

Allah ﷻ may be showing us signs, the food we are now consuming has begun to battle with the nature the human body was originally made with. We are seeing a sharp spike in the number of chronic conditions (31), cancers (32) and other lifestyle related diseases (33). Food is by far not the only contributor, but it is a major component that acts as a stable pillar for the body to repair, heal and communicate.

The topic of food has been made confusing, uncomfortable and frustrating, that even those who may be interested in changing the course of our community's health, give up and live for themselves rather than challenge the status quo and find out the truth. Society has moved so far away from caring about what happens behind the scenes that those who wish to tread the path of a *tayyib* ethical lifestyle are labelled as difficult and abnormal.

Rethink
Can you use steel or glass instead?
Refuse
"May I have some foil instead?" Make a statement.
Recycle
Where is your nearest central drop off point?
Reduce
How much plastic do you really need?
Reuse
Is your plastic safe to use again?
Cancel plastics

Endnotes

1 The Arabic text states:

روى محمد بن مسلم وزرارة أنهما سألا الإمام الباقر عليه السلام، عن أكل لحم الحُمُر الأهلية، فقال: نهى رسول الله صلى الله عليه وآله عن أكلها يوم خيبر، وإنما نهى عن أكلها في ذلك الوقت لأنها كانت حمولة الناس، وإنما الحرام ما حرَّم الله في القرآن

2 The Arabic text states:

وقال الإمام الصادق عليه السلام: سُئل أبي عن لحوم الحمر الأهلية فقال: نهى رسول الله صلى الله عليه وآله عن أكلها لأنها كانت حمولة النـاس يومئذ، وإنما الحرام ما حرم الله في القرآن وإلا فلا

3 The word تنزيه is synonymous to تزكية in يزكيهم as seen in Surah al-Jumuah.

4 The Arabic text states:

روى محمد بن سنان عن أبي الحسن أنه سأله عن ماء الوادي؟ فقال: إن المسلمين شركاء في الماء والنار والكلأ.

5 The Arabic text states:

وروي عن الإمام علي عليه السلام قوله: لا يحل منع الملح والماء.

6 Makarim al-Akhlaq, vol. 2, pg. 180, trad. 2,468. The Arabic text states:

الحِميةُ رأسُ الدواءِ، والمَعِدةُ بيتُ الداءِ، عَوِّدْ بَدَناً ما تَعَوَّدَ

7 www.independent.co.uk/life-style/food-and-drink/ugly-vegetable-food-waste-fruit-vegetable-a8825311.html

Personal Notes

Chapter Three

The Etiquettes of Eating

There are a plethora of commandments and advice about food mentioned in the noble Prophetic tradition and they refer mostly to the following fields:

1. The intention of eating and what is related to piety and purification.

2. The purpose of eating and its relationship to the well-being of a person and his strength.

3. The social aspect of food.

4. The economic dimension to food.

The following is an overview of these fields with the textual sources that are stated about its matter.

One: Food, Piety and Goodness

1. The intention colours a person's acts and the true colour of the believer is the reality of the good intention. His intention of eating food with piety is to gain strength for the obedience to God as mentioned in the verse:

﴿قُلْ إِنَّ صَلاَتِي وَنُسُكِي وَمَحْيَايَ وَمَمَاتِي لِلَّهِ رَبِّ الْعَالَمِينَ ١٦٢﴾

Say: "Indeed, my prayer, my rites of sacrifice, my living and my dying are for Allah, Lord of the worlds." (6:162)

2. The Qur'an prohibits excessive difficulty in matters relating to consumables. So if the purpose of food is for the purpose of gaining strength for worship and servitude of Allah ﷻ there will be no restriction in it as per the verse:

﴿لَيْسَ عَلَى الَّذِينَ آمَنُوا وَعَمِلُوا الصَّالِحَاتِ جُنَاحٌ فِيمَا
طَعِمُوا إِذَا مَا اتَّقَوْا وَآمَنُوا وَعَمِلُوا الصَّالِحَاتِ ثُمَّ اتَّقَوْا
وَآمَنُوا ثُمَّ اتَّقَوْا وَأَحْسَنُوا وَاللَّهُ يُحِبُّ الْمُحْسِنِينَ ٩٣﴾

There is not upon those who believe and do righteousness [any] blame concerning what they have eaten [in the past] if they [now] fear Allah and believe and do righteous deeds, and then fear Allah and believe, and then fear Allah and do good; and Allah loves the doers of good. (5:93)

3. The believer mentions the name of Allah ﷻ at the beginning of eating his food and thanks and praises Allah ﷻ at the end of it. To this end Imam as-Sadiq ؑ said: "When food is placed (on the table) and the name of Allah is mentioned, if Satan says to his companions: 'Go out, there is no share of it (food) with you (to be with the eaters)', he, Satan, would have no share of it with you, but for the one who did not pronounce the name of Allah on his food, Satan has a share with him."[1]

4. Just as Imam as-Sadiq ؑ called toward remembering Allah ﷻ at

the beginning and end of eating, the Prophet Muhammad ﷺ, when he placed his hand on the food, he ﷺ would say:

بِسْمِ اللَّهِ، بَارِكْ لَنَا رَزَقْتَنَا وَعَلَيْكَ خَلْفَهُ

> “I begin in the name of Allah, bless our sustenance for us, and to you is what comes after.

It is also narrated that when Imam as-Sadiq (ع) finished his meal, he would say:

> الحمد لله الذي أطعمنا في جائعين، وسقانا في ظمآنين، وكسانا في عارين، وهدانا في ضالين، وحملنا في راجلين، وآوانا في ضاحين، واخدمنا في عانين وفضّلنا على كثير من العالمين.
>
> All praise and thanks to Allah who fed us in our hunger and gave us to drink during our thirst and clothes us when bare. And guided us during misguidance and carried us when being pedestrian. And was lenient to us during our boisterousness. And attended to us during our struggle. And who favoured us over many amongst the worlds.

5. Because it is possible the dining table could be something thought of as a place of pride and vanity (due to lavishness), it is becoming of the believer to sit at it the sitting of a slave to break within himself the vices of arrogance, excessiveness and selfishness.

Ameer al-Mo’mineen (ع) said: “Take your pure Prophet ﷺ as an example ... until when he continues: Verily he ﷺ would eat (sitting) on the ground and sat the sitting of a servant, fasten his shoes with his hands, patch his garment with his hands, would ride a bare (simple) animal (to get there) and ride behind someone (not arrogant to have lead).”[2]

6. When the believer eats, nothing of his meal remains on his plate

(he does not waste his food) rather he 'licks his plate clean' (leaves no leftovers). Ameer al-Mo'mineen ﷺ said: "Whoever licks clean his plate, the angels pray for him and pray for him to make an ample living and write for him a doubling of good deeds."[3]

7. The same goes for licking clean his fingers after food is also recommended for the believer to do so, as it is narrated that the Prophet ﷺ said: "The one who eats, let him suck clean his fingers for in this is a blessing."[4]

8. The believer gives reverence and appreciation to what Allah ﷻ has blessed him with, be it the bread, wheat or barely and avoids disdaining or lacking gratitude for it. In this regard, Imam as-Sadiq ﷺ was asked about (the permissibility of) praying on a pile of wheat and he forbade, so it was asked of him: "What if it was brushed and spread out (like a mat)?" He replied: "Do not pray your ritual prayer upon anything edible for it is sustenance and a living from Allah for His creation and His blessing upon them. So venerate and respect it (that food stuff) and do not disdain or belittle it, for a community who came before you, Allah made their sustenance ample upon them. They would use the pure breads as a pot (like *afhaar*) and made them to be a means of weighing and measuring by them (a means of trickery and disrespect of their blessing). Thereafter Allah tested them with years of deprivation and hunger and had to eat the bread they were using for (false) weighing. So for them this verse was revealed: 'And Allah sets forth a parable: (Consider) a town safe and secure to which its means of subsistence come in abundance from every quarter; but it became ungrateful to Allah's favours, therefore Allah made it to taste the utmost degree of hunger and fear because of what they wrought.'"[5]

(16:112)

9. The believer spiritually enjoys his food and thanks Allah ﷻ for it and for his wellness and security before he eats, during his food and after it. During the meal, the believer remembers how many graces others have lost or been deprived of and how many have been provided by Allah ﷻ to him - praise and thanks be to Allah ﷻ indeed.

Commentary: How we Eat, Position, Process and Digest

The way in which Allah ﷻ has created this amazing human being is fascinating!

Our digestive process begins at the smell and sight of food.

We begin to produce saliva, our gastric stomach acid starts being produced for breakdown; our parasympathetic nervous system takes over to make us prepared for receiving food and the pancreatic enzymes begin their process of release even though we have not even taken a bite.

'Eating with your eyes', as the saying goes, is hardwired in the brain.

Hence, how we approach eating is as significant as to how we digest and process the food. The posture we hold during eating and the place we choose to eat can all influence the way in which that food nourishes us and digests.

Food takes a journey from the moment it enters our mouths through to the intestines and then excreted, if required.

During that journey the posture that our body holds impacts how easy the food travels.

As an example, if we eat while lying down or slouching, we can make it more difficult for the food to travel down the throat and oesophagus. The person will also be directly impacting the diaphragm. The diaphragm is a strong muscle that sits underneath your rib cage and acts as a 'massager' of the intestines during the process of breathing (figure 2). A slouching or lying down posture

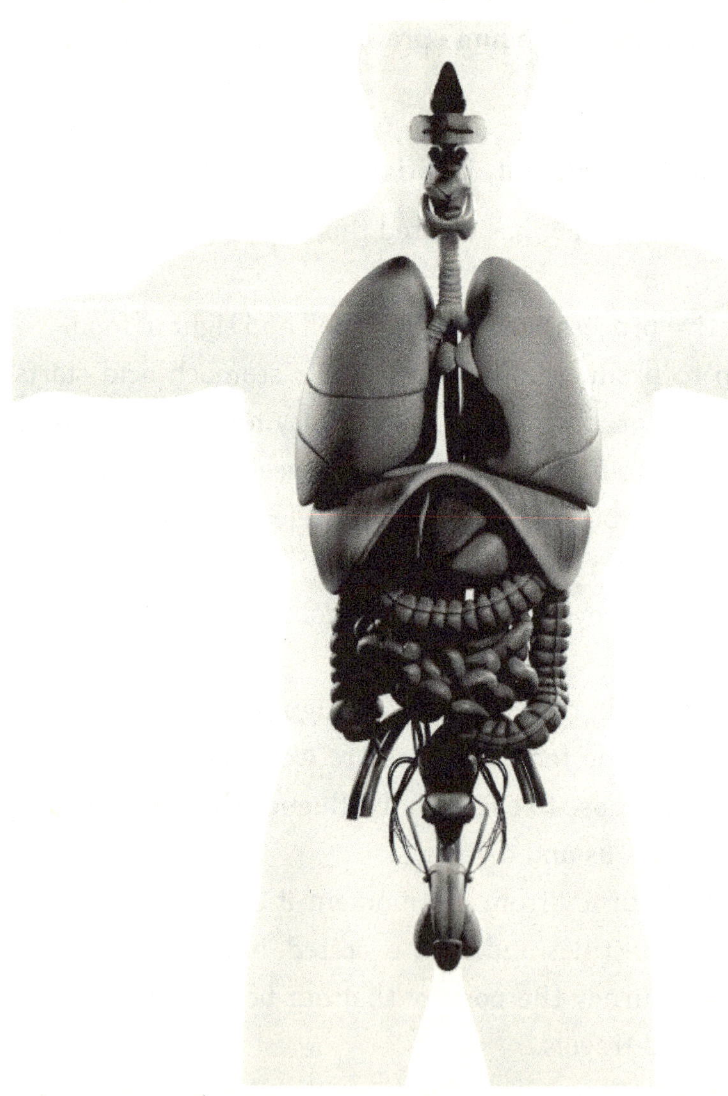

Figure 2

will hinder the benefits the diaphragm provides in moving food through your extremely large intestines.

It is not only the position you choose to sit in, but also the place in which one chooses to eat.

There are studies that show watching TV whilst eating can influence the satiety signals making it hard for the body to know if the person has eaten enough, hence one keeps eating without remembering what they have eaten and how much (34).

Think about the large popcorn box you unexpectedly finished during a film, only to regret it after the show. This is because it takes twenty minutes for your body to recognise that you have eaten a meal and switch off the signals that are telling you that you are hungry (34).

Distractions like the TV can prevent this process of hunger signaling from occurring so that you assume you are hungry but actually you may be quite full.

Reflection Point

Where do you eat your meals? Are there simple steps you could change in the layout of your house that can help to set up a better eating position and environment?

Could you schedule one meal a day that is eaten together as a family?

It is related to the hormone, leptin, produced by fat cells, which communicates with the brain about long-range needs and satiety, based on the body's energy stores. Research suggests that leptin amplifies the satiety signals, to enhance the feeling of fullness.

Other research suggests that leptin also interacts with the neurotransmitter dopamine in the brain to produce a feeling of pleasure after eating.

The theory is that, by eating too quickly, people may not give this intricate hormonal cross-talk system enough time to work. As a result, eating slowly, or rather paying attention to your eating, may help you feel full faster and helps avoiding gluttony.

Paying attention to what and how much one is eating is part of the etiquettes of eating which aid moderation and self-control. This is why the Qur'an says:

﴿فَلْيَنظُرِ ٱلْإِنسَٰنُ إِلَىٰ طَعَامِهِۦٓ ٢٤﴾

"Let the person consider his food."

Imam Ali ﷺ says: "There are four things which when given to someone, they have indeed been given the good of this world and the Hereafter: Truthful speech, fulfilment of trusts, restraint in [filling] one's stomach, and a good nature."[6]

In the same vein the Qur'an links remembering Allah ﷻ, that is being conscious of Him, and the hearts being at ease and in comfort. This is physical as well as spiritual as Imam Ali ﷺ said: "Piety and greed can never come together."[7]

﴿الَّذِينَ آمَنُوا وَتَطْمَئِنُّ قُلُوبُهُم بِذِكْرِ اللَّهِ أَلَا بِذِكْرِ اللَّهِ تَطْمَئِنُّ الْقُلُوبُ ٢٨﴾

Those who believe, and whose hearts find their rest in the remembrance of God - for, verily, in the remembrance of God [men's] hearts do find their rest. (13:28)

Arguably, the state of your mind as you approach food maybe the most important in the process of digestion.

Our mental health, stress, anxiety and thoughts have been shown to physically change the amount of acid production in the stomach, the transit time in your intestines and even the ability for your body to absorb nutrients (35).

The mind-gut connection is accepted as a major player in our health and well-being.

We are aware that we have more neural connections travelling up to the brain from the gut then we do from the brain to the gut (36). The gut is communicating with our brain constantly and giving us information about the health of our body. Our conscious awareness of what we are eating, how we are eating and being present with the meal we are about to have is crucial to our health, a concept prescribed today as 'Mindful Eating'.

This is clearly demonstrated in Islamic texts which asks us to be fully attentive and not on auto-pilot throughout the process of the meal.

For example, Imam al-Hasan ﷺ said, "There are twelve characteristics regarding sitting at a dining-table which each Muslim should learn. Four of them are obligatory, four are recommendable, and four are good manners. The four obligatory characters are knowing what to eat; pronouncing the name of Allah (by saying 'Bismillah'); gratitude; and contentment. The four recommendable characteristics washing before you eat; sitting on the left leg; eating with three fingers; and sucking the fingers. The four characteristics that are good manners are eating only from what is placed before you; taking small bites of food to eat; chewing the food thoroughly; and avoiding staring at other people's faces."[8]

It is my opinion that the focus on traditions discussing how we approach our meals from hand washing to gratitude to position we choose to sit in are not only for spiritual purposes alone, but also have empirical evidence in what we observe in the human body.

What is the Prophetic Sunnah and Tayyib (pure) Order of Eating ?

As can be noted from above, the Prophetic, pure way of eating is vastly detailed. However, the verses and narrations mentioned by Ayatollah al-Modarresi do not draw them together in a sequence that allows the reader to implement them step by step. It is also important to note that one of the most powerful contributions of Ayatollah al-Modarresi in this topic is found in his commentary of Surah al-Waqi'ah.

In this section we present a comprehensive order to the practices a person may wish to adopt for his eating, which would reflect the Tayyib, pure and lofty way of enjoying his meal.

1. The Supplication when the Table Spread is Laid Out

When the table-spread was laid out, the Prophet ﷺ recited:

سُبْحَانَكَ أَللّٰهُمَّ مَا أَحْسَنَ مَا تَبْتَلِينَا، سُبْحَانَكَ مَا أَكْثَرَ مَا تُعْطِينَا، سُبْحَانَكَ مَا أَكْثَرَ مَا تُعَافِينَا، أَللّٰهُمَّ أَوْسِعْ عَلَيْنَا وَ عَلى فُقَرَآءِ الْمُؤْمِنِينَ وَ الْمُؤْمِنَاتِ وَ الْمُسْلِمِينَ وَ الْمُسْلِمَاتِ

Glory be to You O Allah! How wonderful is that which You have tested us with. Glory be to You, how plentiful is that which You have given us. Glory be to You, how plentiful is that which you have bestowed on us. O Allah, increase for us (our sustenance) and for the poor believing men and women and (for the poor) Muslim men and women.

And in another narration, he ﷺ would say:

بِسْمِ اللهِ أَللهمَّ اجْعَلْهَا نِعْمَةً مَشْكُورَةً تَصِلُ بِهَا نِعْمَةَ الْجَنَّةِ

In the Name of Allah! Make it an appreciated blessing by means of which the bounties of paradise are attained.

2. How to Sit and be With People

Ibrahim ibn al-Abbas narrated: "I have never seen Abu al-Hasan (Imam) al-Ridha ﵇ hurt anybody with something he said, nor have I ever seen him interrupt anyone until he had finished, nor refuse someone a favor that he was able to do, or did he ever stretch his legs before anyone sitting with him, nor lean against something while his companion did not, nor did he ever insult any of his servants or workers. And I have never seen him spit or burst into laughter; rather, his laughter was just a smile. When he was ready to eat and the table had been laid, he seated with him at the table all his servants, including the doorman and the stable boy."[9]

3. Beginning in the Name of Allah ﷻ

Imam as-Sadiq ﵇ said: "When food is placed (on the table) and the name of Allah is mentioned, if Satan says to his companions 'Go out, there is no share of it (food) with you (to be with the eaters)', he, Satan, would have no share of it with you, but for the one who did not pronounce the name of Allah on his food, Satan has a share with him.'"

4. Being Grateful to Allah ﷻ for the food

Abu 'Abd Allah as-Sadiq ﵇ said: "The Messenger of Allah ﷺ said: "One who takes food with gratitude has a reward like the one who fasts exercising vigilance over himself. The healthy person grateful for his health has a reward like the one who bears his (bodily) afflictions patiently. And one who gives gratefully has a reward similar to the one who bears his deprivation with continence."[10]

5. Begin With a Pinch of Salt

6. The order of eating

According to Ayatollah al-Modarresi, the order of eating is first to take some drink, then eat greens or fruits, followed by the main meal. This is understood from the sequence of serving a meal in paradise.

﴿عَلَىٰ سُرُرٍ مَّوْضُونَةٍ ۝١٥﴾

They (will be seated) on gold-encrusted couches, (56:15)

﴿مُّتَّكِـِٔينَ عَلَيْهَا مُتَقَٰبِلِينَ ۝١٦﴾

Reclining on them, arrayed face to face; (56:16)

﴿يَطُوفُ عَلَيْهِمْ وِلْدَٰنٌ مُّخَلَّدُونَ ۝١٧﴾

Immortal youths shall go about them (56:17)

﴿بِأَكْوَابٍ وَأَبَارِيقَ وَكَأْسٍ مِّن مَّعِينٍ ۝١٨﴾

With goblets and ewers and a cup filled with a drink drawn from a running spring, (56:18)

﴿لَّا يُصَدَّعُونَ عَنْهَا وَلَا يُنزِفُونَ ۝١٩﴾

A drink by which their minds will not be clouded nor will it cause drunkenness; (56:19)

﴿وَفَٰكِهَةٍ مِّمَّا يَتَخَيَّرُونَ ۝٢٠﴾

They will also go about them with the fruits of which they may choose, (56:20)

﴿وَلَحْمِ طَيْرٍ مِّمَّا يَشْتَهُونَ ﴿٢١﴾﴾

And with the flesh of any fowl that they may desire to eat. (56:21)

7. Not Eating Too Much

The Messenger of Allah ﷺ said: "Do not numb the hearts with excessive eating and drinking for the hearts die like plants do when it receives too much water poured on it" and he ﷺ has also said: "I warn you of the danger of excessively filling your stomachs! For in that is the spoiling of your abdomen, the inheritance of illness and a means of breaking your worship apart."

8. Finishing With a Pinch of Salt

9. Supplication and Thanks Upon Finishing the Meal

When Imam as-Sadiq ؑ finished his meal he would say:

أَلْحَمْدُ لِلَّهِ الَّذِي أَطْعَمَنَا فِي جَائِعِينَ، وَسَقَانَا فِي ظَمَآنِينَ، وَكَسَانَا فِي عَارِينَ، وَهَدَانَا فِي ضَالِينَ، وحملنا في راجلين، وآوانا في ضاجين، واخدمنا في عانين وفضّلنا على كثير من العالمين.

All praise and thanks to Allah who fed us in our hunger and gave us to drink during our thirst and clothes us when bare. And guided us during misguidance and carried us when being pedestrian. And was lenient to us during our boisterousness. And attended to us during our struggle. And who favoured us over many amongst the worlds.

10. Supplication Upon Clearing the Table

In a narration, when the table-spread was picked up the Prophet ﷺ would say:

أَللهمَّ أَكْثَرْتَ وَ أَطَبْتَ وَ بَارَكْتَ فَأَشْبَعْتَ وَ أَرْوَيْتَ، أَلْحَمْدُ للهِ الَّذِي يُطْعِمُ وَ لاَ يُطْعَمُ

O Allah! You have increased Your bounties and made them good and blessed, thereby making us satiated and quenched. Allah praise be to Allah, the One who nourishes and is not nourished.

Second: Food is, by Itself, a Delight and Well-Being

Perhaps the two words "wholesome" and "healthy" reflect a persons's need for immediate pleasure and enjoyment when eating and secondarily health and well-being. Actually, it is upon the person to choose his food well. Firstly, to enjoy it and not to eat like cattle that only aim to fill the stomach and perform physiological functions; and secondly, to benefit by it, the food, in future health, strength and activity.

Thus the believer is being made and remade through the source of the food, his place of dining, his circumstances and his utensils, with its orderliness and beautification without going to the extent of waste, extravagance or luxury.

1. First, that he should eat with his right hand because in the right (hand) is honour and respect. It has been narrated by Imam Ja'far ibn Muhammad as-Sadiq ؑ who said: "A person should not eat with his left hand nor drink with it, nor reach for or take anything (consume) with it except for the one with cause or defect."[11]

2. Second, the believer eats communally (not alone) with his family and friends because the pleasure of eating is greater with people. The Prophet ﷺ said: "The most beloved of food in the eyes of God is the one that has increased upon it the hands of the believers."[12]

Imam Ali ﷺ is narrated to have said: "The more blessed food is the one that has increased due to more sharing of it."[13]

3. Third, he avoids eating in the market place for it has been related by the Prophet ﷺ who said: "Eating in the market places is a low act."[14]

4. Fourth, do not eat food when it is too hot, for it has been related by Imam Ali ibn Abi Talib ﷺ who said: "The Prophet ﷺ came with extremely hot food and said: Allah would not feed us fire (of hell) - so he blew on it until it is became cooler and said 'Food which is extremely hot wipes out the blessings and for Satan therein is a partnership.'"[15]

Imam Ali ﷺ also said: "Blow on hot on food until it becomes cool and edible. Allah would not feed us the fire (of hell) and the blessings lie in it being eaten whilst cool."[16]

5. Fifthly, he prepares and makes his food to high standards, for it has been related from Imam Ja'far al-Sadiq ﷺ who said to some of his companions whilst he was eating with them: "A person can know the love he has for his friend by the quality and generosity of his food. And it greatly pleases me that a person eats from my own food and enjoys the quality and portion of the food. Indeed that pleases me a lot."[17]

Here there are many other deep lessons in the enjoyment of good food gather in the verse:

﴿قُلْ مَنْ حَرَّمَ زِينَةَ اللهِ الَّتِي أَخْرَجَ لِعِبَادِهِ وَالطَّيِّبَاتِ مِنَ الرِّزْقِ قُلْ هِيَ لِلَّذِينَ ءَامَنُوا فِي الْحَيَاةِ الدُّنْيَا خَالِصَةً يَوْمَ الْقِيَامَةِ كَذَلِكَ نُفَصِّلُ الآيَاتِ لِقَوْمٍ يَعْلَمُونَ ﴿٣٢﴾﴾

> Say: 'Who has forbidden the adornment of Allah which He has produced for His servants and the good [lawful] things of provision?' Say: 'They are for those who believe during the worldly life [but] exclusively for them on the Day of Resurrection.' Thus do We detail the verses for a people who know." (7:32)

Thus (we learn that) adornment and the good lawful things (food) are from the sustenance of Allah ﷻ for the believers and for them they can benefit by them fully and completely. As for what is related to matters of good health, a large element of advice from the guidelines of Islam, the teachings of the Qur'an and Prophetic way, are related to it and so we shall present in what is to follow just a few examples only:

a. It is heavily disliked to eat too much until satiation and be bloated just as it is dis-recommended to eat on a full stomach. It has been related that the Messenger of Allah ﷺ said: "Do not numb the hearts with excessive eating and drinking for the hearts die like plants do when it receives too much water poured on it."[18]

The Prophet ﷺ said: "I warn you of the danger of excessively filling your stomachs! For in that is the spoiling of your abdomen, the inheritance of illness and a means of breaking your worship apart."[19]

The Prophet ﷺ has also said: "Whoever gets used to eating food and drinking excessively, his heart hardens."[20]

Ameer al-Mo'mineen ﷺ said: "Whoever excessively eats reduces the quality of his health and brings upon himself the spectre of death."[21]

b. It is recommended to eat a lighter, smaller portion for breakfast and dinner, being the first part of the day and the first part of the night. It has been related by Ali ibn Abi as-Salt that: "I complained to Imam Ja'far as-Sadiq ﷺ about receiving aches and pains. He replied: 'Eat breakfast and dinner but do not eat between them for in that is the corruption of the body. Have you not heard the verse, 'They will have their provision therein, morning and afternoon'?'"[22] (19:62)

It is highly recommended against leaving dinner, especially for the elderly and middle-aged, and it has been narrated by Ja'far ibn Muhammad ﷺ who said: "It is necessary for a person if elder in age, not to go to sleep except having eaten a proper amount of food."[23]

It is recommended to eat something, even if it be as little as bread and salt before leaving the house, and it has been related from Imam as-Sadiq ﷺ who said: "When you have prayed the morning *(fajr)* prayer, eat a morsel by which would give you flavour to your taste (breath), cool yourself down, give healthier gums and strengthen your teeth, bring out by it (the healthy food you eat) your livelihood and improve by it your body. And by these teachings, Islam has organised well the requirements of eating."[24]

1. From amongst the recommendations is the mastery and excellence of food. It is narrated from Imam as-Sadiq ﷺ: "If a person was to spend a thousand dirhams on a certain food and a believer

was to eat from it, it would not be considered a extravagance or a waste."[25]

2. It is also recommended that the dining table or place of eating contains legumes, herbs and greens. It is narrated by Imam as-Sadiq ﷺ: "For everything there is a decoration, and the decoration for a large meal is legumes."[26]

3. It is also recommended to have on the dining table or place, meat. The Messenger of Allah ﷺ said: "The best of foods in this world and the next is the meat."[27]

4. It is recommended to prefer barely bread over wheat. It is narrated by Imam al-Kadhim ﷺ: "The preference of barely bread over wheat is like the excellence of us (the Ahl al-Bayt) over mankind! There has not been a Prophet except that he called towards eating barely and that he blessed it. It (barely) did not enter a stomach except that every ailment and disorder has left it (due to the barely). And so it, the barely bread, is a diet and nourishment for the prophets and food choice of the righteous. And God Almighty would refuse to provide the nourishment of prophets to the wicked."[28]

5. It is also preferable to eat the meat of a well fed, younger lamb. It is narrated: "All the ripe meat of the young lamb is best, not the lengthily treated meat, the elderly sheep yet to be slaughtered and not that of a cow."[29]

It is narrated the Prophet ﷺ said: "Indeed Allah has selected (made it preferred) something from every type of thing and He preferred the young sheep from amongst the types of sheep."[30]

6. There is no problem in eating beef, though dis-recommended. It is related the Prophet ﷺ said: "Whoever eats a fatty bite (or

meal), an illness comes with it into the body and the meat of the cow is an (carries) illness. But from the cow's fat comes a cure and its milk a remedy. And nothing enters the stomach like the fat."[31]

7. It is recommended to eat younger chickens. Imam Ali ﷺ said: "The purest of meats is the meat of the chicks or what is nearly mature."[32]

8. It is also preferable to choose (meat from) the arm and shoulder. The Prophet ﷺ said: "Buy for us the meat from the front parts of the animal and do not buy from the back part. For the meat that is outermost is closest to the pasture and furthest from harm."[33]

9. It is recommended to eat kebab to ward off weakness. It is narrated Imam Musa al-Kadhim ﷺ wrote to Musa bin Bakr al-Wasiti so he came to visit. The Imam ﷺ said: "What is the matter that I see you unwell, yellow faced? Is it not that I told you to eat meat?" Ibn Bakr replied: "I have not missed eating it since you told me." Imam al-Kadhim ﷺ replied: "How have you been eating it?" He replied: "Cooked with food." The Imam said: "Eat it as kebab." Ibn Bakr states that: "So I ate it that way and he wrote again after Friday prayers (to visit) by which time the colour in my face had returned to normal."[34]

10. The same goes for vinegars and oils, that it is recommended to be eaten. It is narrated from Imam as-Sadiq ﷺ: "It is good to have sauces of vinegar and oils for these were favoured by the prophets and chosen as their sauces and are blessed. In fact it is recommended that the house not be free of vinegar and oil."[35]

Imam as-Sadiq ﷺ is narrated to have said: "Keep vinegar and oils in your houses, for no household would become poor whilst keeping them (for they would at least delight the palate)."[36]

11. It is also recommended to eat dates on an empty stomach (morning). The Prophet ﷺ said: "Whoever wakes in the morning and eats dates from *Ajwah* (a type of compressed dates), he will not be harmed that day by poison or magic."[37]

He ﷺ also said: "Eat a date on an empty stomach for it will kill offworms."[38]

12. It is recommended to eat apples and cure yourself by them. Imam as-Sadiq (a) said: "Had people realised what was in apples they would not cure their ailments except by them! They are the fastest thing to benefit the hearts in specific."[39]

13. The same goes for eating chicory and spring onions. For Imam Ali (a) said: "Eat chicory and spring onions, for there is no morning without it being dropped from the paradise itself."[40]

Imam as-Sadiq (a) said: "Whoever eats chicory and spring onions, it is written for him to be among the secure that day and night."[41]

14. It is also recommended to benefit and receive treatment from the medicines in leeks. Imam al-Baqir (a) is narrated to have had a man from his followers complain to him about pain in the spleen area and he had tried every type of remedy, yet his pain was increasing until it reached where he might die. Al-Baqir (a) said: "Purchase with a piece of silver (indicating the cost at that time) and eat a portion of leek. Sautee it well in Arab fat and eat from it for three days for if he was to do that he would be healed by the Will of Allah."[42]

There are many other teachings about the nature and practice of eating where we cannot now deliberate and further examine, but it involves taking care of dining from the perspective of a holistic wellbeing. This is whether it is from the perspective of (different) fruits or herbs, or breads or sauces, which are rich in all the necessary components and minerals needed by the human body which supply him with good health and activity.

D. As for matters regarding the way (etiquettes) and spirit of eating, there are many deep teachings also, of which include the following:

1. Washing of the hands before and after eating. It is narrated from Imam Ali ﷺ: "Whoever washes his hands before and after eating, he will be blessed from the beginning of the meal and in its end."[43]

And the Prophet ﷺ said: "Washing of the hands before and after eating removes poverty and draws sustenance."[44]

And Imam as-Sadiq ﷺ said: "When you wash your hands from eating, wipe them over your face before you wipe them (dry) with a towel and say (the following supplication): O Allah I ask You for adornment and love and seek refuge with you from abomination and wrath."[45]

2. Eating whilst slouching or lying flat is detestable. Imam Ali ﷺ said: "Do not eat slouching as do the mighty and tyrannical nor cross-legged."[46]

Imam as-Sadiq ﷺ also said: "Do not eat slouching and if you are lying down (whilst eating) this is an evil worse than the slouching positions."[47]

3. It is also detestable to raise one leg over another when eating. Imam Ali ﷺ said: "If any of you are sitting to eat, sit the humble sitting of a servant. And do not raise one leg over the other and do

not sit cross-legged for in this sort of practice is the anger of Allah and the loathing of he who is sitting like that."[48]

4. The same detesting goes for eating whilst walking, for Imam as-Sadiq ﷺ said: "Do not eat whilst you are walking except when you are necessitated to do so."[49]

5. It is highly dis-recommended to lie down after eating and raise the right leg over the over. It is said by Imam as-Sadiq ﷺ: "Lying down immediately after being full up will make you fat, not digest well and bring about illness."[50]

Imam ar-Redha ﷺ said: "Whoever wants to ease his digestion, let him (later) lie down after eating on his right side, then turn over to his left side until he falls asleep."[51]

6. It is recommended to begin with salt and finish with it. The Prophet ﷺ said: "Whoever regularly begins his meal with salt and finishes with it, he is cured of seventy two illnesses, and amongst them is leprosy."[52]

7. It is dis-recommended to blow on food. Imam Ali ﷺ said: "The Prophet ﷺ prohibited four types of blowing: In the position of prostration; urination and defecation; during eating; and drinking."[53]

It is also preferable whilst eating to avoid eating from the top of the food (from the middle or top of the shared plate), instead eating from what is closest to you or in front of the person.

The Prophet ﷺ said: "If you are eating porridge ("Al-Thareed", breadcrumbs with broth - a type of food from the period of pre-Islam), eat from all sides for in what is on top has blessings."[54]

(The top of the dish usually contains the toppings such as the meat and the chicken etc..so if a person ate from the top directly, the blessings won't be shared by everyone, however, if each person ate from what is in front of him or the sides of the shared dish, each person would get a share of the blessings.)

The Prophet ﷺ said: "When you set the dining table, one should eat from what is in front of him and not stand up nor make a gesture that shows you've finished eating if you're full up until others have stood up or gestured they're finished (do not rush others to finish), otherwise that is stinginess in the rights of his sitting."[55]

8. One should eat with three fingers. The Prophet ﷺ said: "Eating with one finger is the eating of Satan; with two fingers is the eating of the haughty; while eating with three fingers is the eating of the prophets, peace be upon them."[56]

9. It is recommended to pick or brush your teeth after eating. The Prophet ﷺ said: "Pick and clean away the remains of the food for in this is the health of the teeth and it draws sustenance to the servant (of Allah)."[57]

The Prophet ﷺ said: "Clean your mouths with a toothpick for this is the dwelling place of the two writers of deeds (angels). Its saliva is their ink and their pen is the tongue and there is nothing tougher for them to bear than the leftovers of food in the mouth."[58]

10. It is recommended to wash the mouth with as-Sa'ad (a type of herb with medical usage used as a soap) after eating (for fragrance and cleanliness) for when he would perform his ablution (Wudhu') Imam al-Baqir ؑ would gargle his mouth with soap.[59]

11. It is recommended to wash the outside of the mouth with soap.

Third: Food as a Positive Social Link

Food is comfort for ones self and it is spread by necessity and decrease. Thus it is an opportunity for social relationships be it with the family unit or external relations. Here, Islam disciplines, trains and refines believers with a set of good values and customs about food to increase their social ties and strengths between them. From amongst these values are:

a. It is dis-recommended for a person to eat on his own. It is narrated the Prophet ﷺ cursed (prayed for Allah to keep away His Mercy on) three people: the one who ate on his own; the one who rides through a vast barren land alone; and the one who sleeps alone.[60]

b. It is highly recommended for people to gather for food to eat together. The Prophet ﷺ said: "The most beloved of food for Allah, is what gathered upon it the many hands of the believers."[61]

Imam Ali ؑ said: "The food with most blessings is the one with a copious number of hands upon it (the food with more people sharingit)."[62]

c. It is strongly recommended to convey invite to guests and to be hospitable to them. Imam Ali ؑ said: "Indeed from amongst the peaks of good characteristics is conveying invites to guests."[63]

d. It is also recommended to respond to the invite of a believer. The Prophet ﷺ said: "Whoever does not respond to an invite has disobeyed Allah and His Messenger."[64]

e. It is extremely recommended to feed people. Imam Ali ؑ said: "Gathering my companions to eat even a small portion or two, is more beloved to me than leaving your Souq (markets) and freeing a person."[65]

In addition, Imam as-Sadiq ﷺ said, "Feeding a believer is equal to freeing a slave."[66]

f. It is recommended to feed a believer even a morsel. It is narrated by the Prophet ﷺ: "Whoever feeds into the mouth of his believing brother a sweet morsel, free of desiring it to be a bribe and not fearing by it any evil (he has done to it), and not seeking anything other than the pleasure of God the Most High, Allah would turn away from him (because of it) the bitterness of the situation on the Day of Judgement."[67]

g. It is recommended for the people of a town to host guests - those visiting them from amongst their brothers (in the community). The Prophet ﷺ said: "If a person enters a land he is considered a guest for those residing in it from amongst his faith until he departs from them. And it is not correct for a guest to fast except with their (his hosts) permission lest they prepare something for him and it goes to waste or against their plans. Nor is it proper that his hosts should fast except with his permission lest they he feels shy (worried about his intrusion) from them and decides to leave their place."[68]

h. It is recommended to honour and revere the guest. For the Prophet ﷺ said, "Whoever believes in Allah and the Day of Judgement, let him honour his guest." [69]

While Imam Ali ﷺ said, "Honour your guest even if he be contemptible."[70]

Commentary: On Guests and Eating with Others

There are many spiritual benefits outlined by Ayatollah al-

Modarresi regarding eating with others and having guests. Imam al-Ridha ﷺ has a reflective hadith about the generous person where he says: "The generous person partakes of other people's food in order that they may feel comfortable to partake of his food, whereas the miser does not partake of others' food so that they may not eat from his."[71]

To add a physical angle to these spiritual benefits, eating alone versus eating with others may have an impact on the nutrient intake you consume. Those who eat alone seem to drop below the recommended nutrition intake compared to those who eat with others (43).

It is no surprise then the Prophet Muhammad ﷺ is narrated to have said, "A most beloved thing to Allah is to see the believer with his wife and child together on the table eating such than when they gather together to do so, Allah looks upon them with overwhelming Mercy and forgives them their sins before they separate (finish the meal)."[72]

From our previous discussions of the necessity of nutrients for processes in the body, like energy production, we understand that a lack of nutrients can have serious effects on how your body functions.

It is important to note, a nutrient depleted diet can be a very large meal, but a nutrient rich diet doesn't necessarily mean that the meal is grand. Many a time we are confused by quantity versus quality. In order to benefit from nutrients, we need to be consuming the right ingredients, fresh and wholesome in nature.

Our brothers and sisters who are suffering in poverty do not need quantity of food alone, they need good quality food that allows their bodies to function optimally, even if the quantity they receive is just adequate for their household.

Next time you want to provide a homeless person with food, think about what we can give to them. Society has made it cheaper to provide unhealthy meals than healthy and often a homeless person will sit outside a fast food restaurant thinking this might be an easy way to receive quick meals from people already spending their money. We are in fact providing them the least nutrition when they are often in need of it the most, fighting the cold and rain and trekking many miles to find shelter.

Reflection Point

Reflect on those who are less fortunate than us. Those who are homeless, live in poverty or struggling through oppression and war. How are their bodies being able to function? How susceptible are they to disease and infection? What are their daily meal times like?

We live in an era where we take family meal times for granted. Parents and children eat when they want, there is no time for discussion or conversation and the cook (usually the mother) is left cleaning after everyone at the end of the day.

An important study (44) discusses the elderly who eat alone yet live with others, even though there are family within the house they are not eating with them. The authors conclude that encouraging the elderly to eat with others may be a protective measure to prevent early mortality.

One of the significant reasons may relate to the fact that eating with others helps with anxiety, stress and emotions. In younger individuals who suffer from eating disorders and mental health complaints, creating meal times whereby family, friends and community are eating together may be extremely beneficial. Not to mention, eating with others boosts positive chemicals and hormones, brings laughter and draws out conversation and listening skills.

All the family develops together, benefitting each other.

Eat the Rainbow

Use the chart below to measure how much of each colour group you're eating daily.

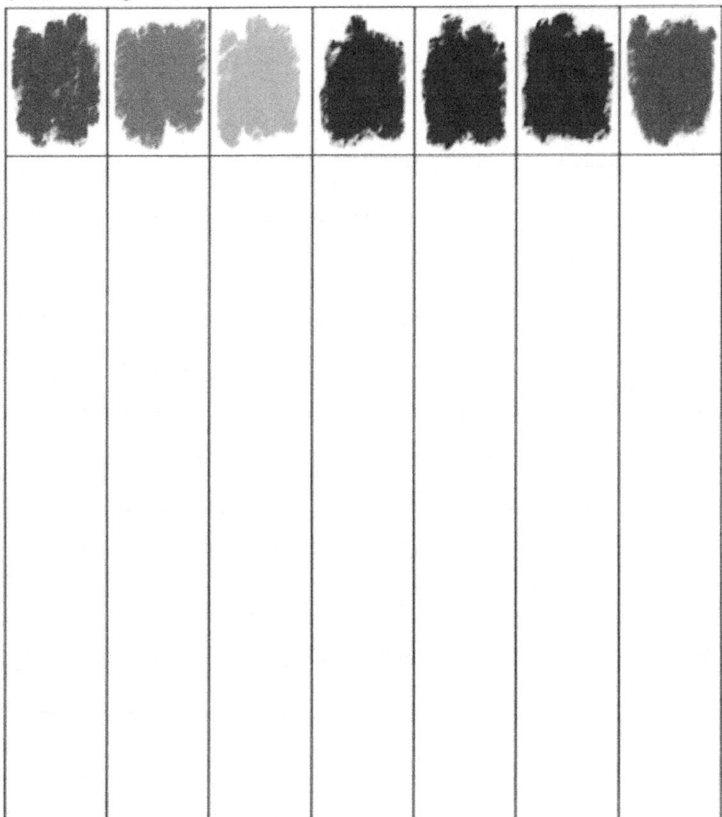

The above colours, from left to right, are:

Red, Orange, Yellow, Green, Blue, Indigo, Violet

Endnotes

1 The Arabic text states:

إذا وضع الطعام فسمّوا، فإن الشيطان يقول لأصحابه أُخرجوا فليس لكم فيه نصيب، ومن لم يُسمِّ على طعامه، كان للشيطان معه فيه نصيب

2 The Arabic text states:

قال: ولقد كان صلى الله عليه وآله يأكل على الأرض ، ويجلس جلسة العبد، ويخصف بيده نعله، ويرقع بيده ثوبه، ويركب الحمار العاري ويردف خلفه

3 The Arabic text states:

من لعق قصعته صلّت عليه الملائكة، ودعت له بالسعة في الرزق، ويكتب له حسنات مضاعفة.

4 The Arabic text states:

من أكل طعاماً فليمص أصابعه فإن في مص أحدها بركة.

5 The Arabic text states:

فإذا افترش وكان على السطح؟ لا يصلى على شيء من الطعام، فإنما هو رزق الله لخلقه ونعمته عليهم، فعظّموه ولا تهاونوا به فإن قوماً ممن كان قبلكم وسع الله عليهم في أرزاقهم، فاتخذوا من الخبز النقي مثل الافهار فجعلوا يستنجون به، فابتلاهم الله عز وجل بالسنين والجوع فجعلوا يتتبعون ما كانوا يستنجون به فيأكلونه وفيهم نزلت هذه الآية: وَضَرَبَ اللَّهُ مَثَلاً قَرْيَةً كَانَتْ ءَامِنَةً مُّطْمَئِنَّةً يَأْتِيهَا رِزْقُهَا رَغَداً مِن كُلِّ مَكَانٍ فَكَفَرَتْ بِأَنْعُمِ اللَّهِ فَأَذَاقَهَا اللَّهُ لِبَاسَ الْجُوعِ وَالْخَوْفِ بِمَا كَانُوا يَصْنَعُونَ

6 Ghurar al-Hikm, Trad. 2,142. The Arabic text states:

أربَعٌ مَن أُعْطِيَهُنَّ فَقَد أُعْطِيَ خَيرَ الدُّنيا والآخِرَة: صِدقُ حَديثٍ، وأداءُ أمانَةٍ، وعِفَّةُ بَطْنٍ، وحُسنُ خُلقٍ.

7 Ibid. Trad. 10,578. The Arabic text states:

لا يَجتَمِعُ الوَرَعُ والطَّمَعُ.

8 Al-Khisal, as-Sadooq, Chapter on the Number Twelve, Hadith no. 61.

9 Uyun al-Akhbar al-Rida, as-Sadooq, Vol. 2, Pg. 184, Trad. 7

10 The Arabic text states:

عَـنْ أَبِي عَبْدِاللـهِ عَلَيْـهِ السَّـلامُ قَـالَ: قَـالَ رَسُـولُ اللـهِ صَ: الطَّاعِـمُ الشَّـاكِرُ لَـهُ مِـنَ الأَجْـرِ كَأَجْـرِ الصَّائِـمِ المُحْتَسِـبِ. وَالمُعَـافَى الشَّـاكِرُ لَـهُ مِـنَ الأَجْـرِ كَأَجْـرِ المُبْتَـلى الصَّابِـرِ. وَالمُعْطَـى الشَّـاكِرُ لَـهُ مِـنَ الأَجْـرِ كَأَجْـرِ المَحْـرومِ القَانِـعِ.

11 The Arabic text states:

لا يأكل الرجل بشماله ولا يشرب بها ولا يتناول بها إلا من علّة

12 The Arabic text states:

أحب الطعام إلى الله ماكثرت عليه أيدي المؤمنين

13 The Arabic text states:

أكثر الطعام بركة ماكثرت عليه الأيدي.

14 The Arabic text states:

الأكل في السوق دناءة

15 The Arabic text states:

أُتي النبـي صـلى اللـه عليـه وآلـه بطعـام حـار جـداً، فقـال صـلى اللـه عليـه وآلـه: مـا كان اللـه ليطعمنـا النـار، اقـروه حتـى يسـكن (ظ) فـإن الطعـام الحـار جـداً ممحـوق البركـة، للشـيطان فيـه شرك

16 The Arabic text states:

اقروا الحار حتى يبرد ويمكن أكله، ما كان الله ليطعمنا النار، والبركة في البارد

17 The Arabic text states:

يعـرف مـودة الرجـل لأخيـه بجـودة أكلـه، وأنـه ليعجبنـي الرجـل يـأكل مـن طعامـي فيجيـد في الأكل، يـسرني بذلـك

18 The Arabic text states:

لا تميتوا القلوب بكثرة الطعام والشراب، فإن القلوب تموت كالزرع إذا كثر عليه الماء.

19 The Arabic text states:

وقـال صـلى اللـه عليـه وآلـه: إياكـم والبطنـة، فإنهـا مفسـدة البطـن ومورثـة للسـقم، ومكسـلة عـن العبـادة.

20 The Arabic text states:

وعن النبي صلى الله عليه وآله أيضاً قال: من تعوّد كثرة الطعام والشراب قسى قلبه

21 The Arabic text states:

وعـن أمـير المؤمنـين عليـه السـلام قـال: مـن كـثر أكلـه، قلـت صحتـه، وثقلـت عـلى نفسـه موتـه.

22 The Arabic text states:

عـن عـلي بـن أبي الصلـت ابـن اخـي شـهاب بـن عبـد ربـه قـال: شـكوت إلى أبي عبـد اللـه عليـه السـلام مـا ألقـى مـن الأوجـاع والتخـم، فقـال: تغـد وتعـش ولا تـأكل بينهـما، فـإن فيـه فسـاد البـدن، أمـا سـمعت اللـه عـز وجـل يقـول: (وَلَهُـمْ رِزْقُهُـمْ فِيهَـا بُكْـرَةً وَعَشِـيّاً((مريـم/٦٢)

23 The Arabic text states:

ويكـره تـرك العشـاء خصوصـاً للشـيخ والكهـل، فقـد روي عـن جعفـر بـن محمـد عليهـما السـلام، أنـه قـال: وينبغـي للرجـل إذا سـن أن لا يبيـت إلا وجوفـه مملـؤ طعامـاً.

24 The Arabic text states:

روي عـن أبي عبـد اللـه عليـه السـلام أنـه قـال: إذا صليـت الفجـر فـكل كـسرة تطيـب بهـا نكهتـك، وتطفـى بهـا حرارتـك، وتقـوم بهـا أضراسـك، وتشـد بهـا لثتـك، وتجلـب بهـا رزقـك، وتحسـن بهـا خلقـك وبهـذه التعاليـم نظـم الإسـلام وجبـات الطعـام.

25 The Arabic text states:

روي عـن الصـادق عليـه السـلام قـال: لـو أن رجـلاً أنفـق عـلى طعـام ألـف درهـم وأكل منـه مؤمـن ، لم يعـد سرفـاً.

26 The Arabic text states:

قال أبو عبد الله عليه السلام: لكل شيء حلية، وحلية الخوان البقل

27 The Arabic text states:

قال رسول الله صلى الله عليه وآله: سيد طعام الدنيا والآخرة اللحم.

28 The Arabic text states:

روي عـن أبي الحسـن عليـه السـلام، قـال: فضـل خبـز الشـعير عـلى الـبرُ كفضلنـا عـلى النـاس، مـا مـن نبـي إلا وقـد دعـا لأكل الشـعير وبـارك عليـه، ومـا دخـل جوفـاً إلا وقـد خـرج كل داء فيـه، وهـو قـوت الأنبيـاء وطعـام الأبـرار، أبى اللـه أن يجعـل قـوت الأنبيـاء للأشـقياء

29 The Arabic text states:

كُلِ اللحم النضيج من الضأن الفتى أسمنه، لا القديد ولا الجزور ولا البقر.

30 The Arabic text states:

إن الله عز وجل اختار من كل شيء شيئاً (إلى إن قال): واختار من الغنم الضأن.

31 The Arabic text states:

مـن أكل لقمـة سـمينة نـزل مـن الـداء مثلهـا مـن جسـده ولحـم البقـر داء وسـمنها شـفاء ولبنهـا دواء، ومـا دخـل الجـوف مثـل السـمن

32 The Arabic text states:

أطيب اللحم، لحم فراخ نهض أو كاد ينهض

33 The Arabic text states:

اشـتر لنـا مـن اللحـم المقاديـم ولا تشـتر المآخـير، فـإن المقاديـم أقـرب مـن المرعـى وأبعـد مـن الأذى

34 The Arabic text states:

قـال: أرسـل إلي أبـو الحسـن عليـه السلام فأتيتـه، فقـال: مـالي أراك مصفـراً؟ وقـال: ألم آمـرك بـأكل اللحـم؟ فقلـت: مـا أكلـت غـيره منـذ أمرتنـي، فقـال: كيـف تأكلـه؟ قلـت: طبيخـاً، قـال: كلـه كبابـاً، فأكلـت، فأرسـل إلي بعـد جمعـة، فـإذا الـدم قـد عـاد في وجهـي.

35 The Arabic text states:

نعم الادام الخل ، ونعم الادام الزيت، وهو طيب الأنبياء وإدامهم وهو مبارك.

36 The Arabic text states:

وأدمنوا الخل والزيت في منازلكم، فما افتقر أهل بيت كان ذلك ادمهم

37 The Arabic text states:

من أصبح بتمرات من عجوة، لم يضره ذلك اليوم سم ولا سحر

38 The Arabic text states:

كلوا التمر على الريق فإنه يقتل الدود

39 The Arabic text states:

لـو يعلـم النـاس مـا في التفـاح مـا داووا مرضاهـم إلا بـه، وإنـه أسرع شيء منفعـة للفـؤاد، خاصـة

40 The Arabic text states:

كل الهندباء، فما من صباح إلا ويقـطر عليه من قطر الجنة

41 The Arabic text states:

من أكل الهندباء كُتب من الآمنين يومه ذلك وليلته

42 The Arabic text states:

انه شكا إليه رجل من أوليائه وجع الطحال، وقد عالجه بكل علاج، وانه يزداد كل يوم شراً، حتى أشرف على الهلكة، فقال عليه السلام: اشتر بقطعة فضة كراث، واقله قلياً جيداً بسمن عربي، وأطعم من به هذا الوجع ثلاثة أيام فإنه إذا فعل ذلك برىء إن شاء الله تعالى .

43 The Arabic text states:

من غسل يديه قبل الطعام وبعده بورك له في أول الطعام وآخره

44 The Arabic text states:

غسل اليدين قبل الطعام وبعده ينفي الفقر ويجلب الرزق

45 The Arabic text states:

إذا غسلت يدك من الطعام فامسح بهما وجهك من قبل أن تمسحهما بالمنديل، وقل: اللهم اني أسألك الزينة والمحبة وأعوذ بك من المقت والمغضبة

46 The Arabic text states:

عن علي صلوات الله عليه ، أنه قال: لا تأكل متكئاً كما يأكل الجبارون، ولا تربع .

47 The Arabic text states:

وعن الصادق عليه السلام، أنه قال: لا تأكل متكئاً، وان كنت منبطحاً هو شر من الاتكاء

48 The Arabic text states:

إذا جلس أحدكم على الطعام فليجلس جلسة العبد، ولا يضعن أحدكم إحدى رجليه على الأخرى، ولا يتربع فانها جلسة يبغضها الله عز وجل، ويمقت صاحبها

49 The Arabic text states:

لا تأكل وأنت ماش، إلا أن تضطر إلى ذلك

50 The Arabic text states:

الاستلقاء بعد الشبع يسمن البدن، ويمرئ الطعام

51 The Arabic text states:

ومن أراد أن يستمرء طعامه فليستلق بعد الأكل على شقه الأيمن، ثم ينقلب على شقه الأيسر حتى ينام

52 The Arabic text states:

من افتتح طعامه بالملح وختم به عوفي من اثنين وسبعين داء، منها الجذام

53 The Arabic text states:

أن رسـول اللـه صـلى الله عليـه وآلـه نهـى عـن أربـع نفخـات ؛ في موضـع السـجود، وفي الرقـا، وفي الطعـام، والـشراب

54 The Arabic text states:

إذا أكلتم الثريد فكلوا من جوانبه، فإن الذروة فيها البركة

55 The Arabic text states:

إذا وضعـت المائـدة فليـأكل أحدكـم مـما يليـه ولا يقـوم أحدكـم ولا يرفـع يـده وان شـبع حتـى يرفـع القـوم أيديهـم فـإن ذلـك يخجـل جليسـه

56 The Arabic text states:

الأكل بإصبـع واحـد أكل الشـيطان، وبالاثنـين أكل الجبابـرة، وبالثـلاث أكل الأنبيـاء عليهـم السـلام

57 The Arabic text states:

تخللوا على أثر الطعام، فإنه صحة للناب والنواجذ ويجلب على العبد الـرزق

58 The Arabic text states:

نقـوا أفواهكـم بالخـلال، فإنـه مسـكن الملكـين الحافظـين الكاتبـين، وان مدادهـما الريـق وقلمهـما اللسـان، وليـس شيء أشـد عليهـما مـن فضـل الطعـام في الفـم

59 The Arabic text states:

أنه كان إذا توضأ بالأشنان ادخله فاه فتطاعمه ثم رمى به

60 The Arabic text states:

أنه لعن ثلاثة؛ آكل زاده وحده، وراكب الفلاة وحده، والنائم في بيت وحده

61 The Arabic text states:

أحب الطعام إلى الله ما كثرت عليه أيدي المؤمنين

62 The Arabic text states:

أكثر الطعام بركة ما كثرت عليه الأيدي

63 The Arabic text states:

إن من مكارم الأخلاق إقراء الضيف

64 The Arabic text states:

من لم يجب الدعوة ، فقد عصى الله ورسوله

65 The Arabic text states:

لأن اجمع نفراً من إخواني على صاع أو صاعين، احب إلي من أن اخرج إلى سوقكم هذه فاعتق نسمة

66 The Arabic text states:

إطعام مؤمن يعدل عتق رقبة

67 The Arabic text states:

من أُلقم في فم أخيه المؤمن لقمة حلو لا يرجو لها رشوة ولا يخاف بها من شره، ولا يريد إلا وجهه تعالى، صرف الله عنه بها مرارة الموقف يوم القيامة

68 The Arabic text states:

إذا دخل رجل بلدة فهو ضيف على من بها من أهل دينه حتى يرحل عنهم، ولا ينبغي للضيف أن يصوم إلا بإذنهم لئلا يعملوا له الشيء، فيفسد عليهم، ولا ينبغي لهم أن يصوموا إلا بإذنه لئلا يحتشمهم فيترك لمكانهم

69 The Arabic text states:

من كان يؤمن بالله واليوم الآخر فليكرم ضيفه

70 The Arabic text states:

اكرم ضيفك وإن كان حقيراً

71 The Arabic text states:

قال الامام الرضا (ع) السخيُّ يأكلُ من طعامِ الناس ليأكلوا من طعامه ، و البخيلُ لا يأكلُ من طعام الناسِ لئلّا يأكلوا من طعامه

72 The Arabic text states:

أحب شيء إلى الله تعالى: أن يرى المؤمن مع امرأته وولده على مائدة يأكلون، فإذا اجتمعوا عليها نظر الله إليهم بالرحمة والمغفرة، ويغفر لهم قبل أن يتفرقوا

Personal Notes

Chapter Four

Food and its Relation to Organising Life and Livelihood

It is upon a person to balance and organise well his livelihood and to care about his food within his capabilities such that he does not undertake (things) which he is not capable of. Allah ﷻ has provided most of man's needs in food such that the believer can manage himself without difficulty or burdening himself and without being harmed by anything. In this remit there are numerous points of learning as follows:

a. It is highly recommended for a person to appreciate his food as much as possible. Imam as-Sadiq ﷺ said, "There should be no wastage in food."[1]

b. It is normal that hosting guests is a cost and extra responsibility when it comes to food. Islam however disallows this rather encouraging the guest not to burden his host in anything.

It is narrated from Imam al-Hussain ﷺ that he said: "Imam Ali ﷺ called a person (to his house) and said to him, 'Should I give you three things you are responsible to me toward (as my guest)?" The man replied, 'What are those?' Imam replied, 'Do not bring anything to me from outside (eg your own food); do not stash away anything of mine from the house; and do not prejudice against anyone of the family.'"[2]

From another perspective it is highly recommended for a guest not to belittle what is offered to him from the blessings of Allah. The Prophet ﷺ said, "Whoever scorns what his brother offers him, he will not be relieved of the hate of Allah that day or night."[3]

It is also recommended not to be ashamed before him (the guest). The Prophet ﷺ said, "Uphold the highest morals of the prophets, the truthful, the martyrs and righteous when visiting one another in the way of Allah. And it is the right of the host to bring to his guest what would is easy and available for him, even if it be as little as a sip of water. But whoever is ashamed to bring to his guest what he is capable of, he will not be relieved of the hate of Allah that day or night."[4]

c. It is not permissible for a person to use food for seeking pretension, hypocrisy and reputation, such as something which usually costs him well beyond his capacity. The Prophet ﷺ said, "Whoever feeds people for the sake of being admired, seen or heard about, Allah will feed him from the puss of hell and make that food as fire in his belly until the matter is settled between people on the Day of Judgement."[5]

d. And perhaps it is easy to overlook the issue of wastage and lavishness when serving food. Thus, it is mentioned in Islamic teachings to pay attention to this matter such that it is extremely disliked to even throw away fruits before checking properly if they are edible or not ripe or have gone bad. Imam as-Sadiq ؑ is narrated to have seen a discarded fruit in his house not checked for its ripeness and readiness to be eaten and so he became angry. He asked, "What's this?! If you are full up and don't need to eat any more then know there are plenty of people who are not! Feed to whoever needs it."[6]

And it is preferable that when fresh bread is made or brought in that you not wait for others things before eating. Imam Ali ﷺ said, "Honour the bread for Allah the Most High has brought down the blessing from heaven to it." It was asked "What is meant by honouring it?" to which he ﷺ replied, "If it is present, fresh, do not wait for other things to eat it."[7]

And it is recommended to cut the loaf thinly or reduce the size of the bread for the Prophet ﷺ said, "Make small the slices of your loaves for in every slice is a blessing."[8]

We ask Allah to grant us success in seeking a deep understanding of the religion and to benefit and utilise its teachings which enliven the heart and body. Indeed He is the Master of success.

Commentary: Emotions and Food

Over centuries, from the ancient civilisations to the current time, we have seen a shift in our relationship with food. Food used to be consumed for survival in past generations. They would eat to live, to survive and replenish for the next day's work. If there were any emotional attachments to food it would have been one of success and of gratefulness. Every morsel and crumb would be looked after and honoured as sustenance that acknowledges life.

Today we are bombarded with a variety of choices and advertisements. Our natural understanding of differentiating between friendly nutritious food and potentially harmful foods has become inert.

We are taught to believe that our cereal boxes provide the same nutrients as the grain we used to pick with our bare hands, yet hidden inside our cereal boxes are increased levels of refined sugar, fillers and preservatives.

What most people never realise is that the commercial industry has mastered the engineering of foods to keep us addicted, constantly craving more of whatever falsely satisfying manufactured treat is in front of us. Foods that aren't naturally sweet are artificially sweetened to keep consumers craving the product, with sugar levels that can rival those found in packaged desserts.

Reflection Point
Top tips for choosing food at a supermarket: Check the ingredients, if it has more than 5 ingredients then know that it is a processed food. A carrot just has a carrot, it's a good place to start.

Salt too, is extremely addictive, just as much as sugar. The more you consume salt, the more you crave it, and manufacturers realise this, leaving the consumer in a vicious cycle.

Studies demonstrate sugar's addictive qualities, suggesting that it can, in some circumstances, lead to behaviour and neurochemical changes that resemble the effects of substance abuse. This according to Jeffrey Sachs, director of the Center for Sustainable Development at Columbia University, is a sign of the broken food system we inhabit.

Eating too much salt is damaging to health because the extra water that you hold on to raises your blood pressure. The more salt you eat, the higher your blood pressure and all of this can put a strain on your heart, kidneys, brain and arteries, which could lead to a stroke, heart attack or kidney disease. Yet many remain casually addicted to this.

Ever wondered why there has to be a label stating 'with added vitamins' on a cereal box? Aren't natural foods supposed to be optimal in the level of nutrients they provide? Maybe this is why Allah ﷻ has linked the foods of paradise with natural sweetness and sugars we crave so we need not seek them artifically.

Imam as-Sadiq ؑ said: "There are five heavenly fruits in this world. They are: pomegranates, apples, quince, grapes and ripe dates."[9]

We are at a stage in life that many researchers say even the levels of nutrients inside our naturally grown fruits and vegetables are deplete, and in order to reach optimal levels we are all in need of supplementation.

Even with this knowledge, most of us will go back to our old ways and avoid the topic of food all together. As a result, food plays havoc with our emotions. In fact, companies like Pringles hire researchers to find out the exact levels of salt and sugar that would stimulate your brains emotional centres and release enough dopamine that would make you want to consume more of them, not less and not more but just enough (16). This explains the infamous marketing slogans like, "Once you pop, you just can't stop," and "Betcha can't eat just one!" It is not because they naturally taste so good, but rather, they are *literally* addictive, that is why you *cannot* stop!

Because their share prices depend on our addictions, our cultures thrive off food. Food is used for social gatherings, for community events, weddings, business meetings; worse still to snack and binge eat on. It has become so in-grained in our nature that we have developed the fear of not pleasing someone or being displeased ourselves if the dining spread is lacking in flavour, quantity or presentation. Our meals are no longer complete if they do not have every palate of dishes on the table, even if this means we cook too much to eat and often much goes to waste.

How the food was prepared, the journey it has gone through and the quality of nutrients in the food is secondary and sometimes not even a concern. Should we not take pride in where the seed was planted, how God made it grow and the way in which it was treated, picked and prepared. I refer back to our previous reflection, could this be having impact on our human nature?

Choices Have Confused Us

Eating has not become easier, even with the advent of supermarkets. With the number of choices placed in front of us it has become more difficult to choose the more preferable sources of nutrition.

Take a step back and reflect on the copious amount of food and choice just one aisle of the supermarket has.

Cereal, principally, is of four types: Wheat, oats, rye and barley. Yet in 2012, in the U.S. there were some 4,945 types of cereal a person could purchase! The era of mass customisation has given every kind flavour, style and preference a person can imagine. Compare this availability and greed with the catastrophic situation in Yemen, a country which due to war upon it from Saudi Arabia, the U.S. and Britain - the world's super powers - is mired in the world's worst humanitarian crisis.

What does all of this variety and greed do to us? Does it keep us free human beings or enslaved, where our eyes are bigger than our stomachs, unashamedly unaware of the needs of those beyond our own fridge?

Imam Ali ﷺ replies by stating, "Whoever wishes to spend the days of his life as a free man must not allow greed to abide in his heart."

It is not a coincidence that the sale items are kept at the entrance of the store and they happen to always be extremely unhealthy. From fizzy drinks, sugary snacks to crisps and quick ready meals. Whilst reading this you may be thinking that this is 'normal', but this is far from normal, it has become normalised over time. Our understanding of how food is grown and where it comes from is starting to disappear. If we ask our children how cocoa is made in their chocolate bars, they will probably answer by saying in a 'Cadbury' factory and not from child slavery!

Advertising has added to the mixture of the confusion with the use of enticing colours, labels, pictures, words, jingles and slogans.

As mentioned in a previous example, if we mention the word 'vitamins' in brightly coloured letters it will immediately catch your attention for its health benefits.

Next time we take a walk around the supermarket, spend a few seconds reading the labels of 'healthy' labelled products. The best example is granola, known to us as a healthy cereal option. You see the rolled oats with added dried fruit on the packet, that is colourfully labelled for vibrancy and morning energy. But take a look at the ingredients, usually the second ingredient is sugar, 25g per 100g of it. To put this into context, research found that the cereal with the highest sugar content had 71.25% of a child's daily allowance of sugar in a 30g bowl while a supermarket branded cereal had 27% of a child's daily dose in a 30g bowl. This heavily impacts childhood obesity.

This Greed has Led to Hoarding

The 2020 global pandemic led to scenes across Western countries of empty shelves and people fighting to stock up on everything from flour and soap to toilet paper to sugar.

Panic buying is a symptom of a dysfunctional society, pervaded with individualism and short term thinking. Those who buy up packs of disinfectant in the hope to slow the transmission of Covid-19 were aware that others need it just as much, yet do not consider their needs as equal to their own. This is a reflection of the political, economic and moral systems we live in, which have produced people who think and act in this way.

Islamic Law has since its inception included the topic of monopolisation and price-fixing called al-Ihtikar.

Ayatollah Muhammad Jawad Mughniyyah states: "The Muslim community have in their entirety agreed on the prohibition of monopolisation as an idea; this is from textual evidence and it being rationally abhorrent in the principle of organising life in such a way that repels harm from being occasioned, from the prohibition of greed and wrongfully withholding, is rationally indigent, looked down upon, and goes against the right of maintaining ones honour and the command of being soft hearted.

"And even if we were to close our eyes to (the principles of) honour and soft heartedness, there would be upon us numerous religious principles which would necessitate the prohibition of monopoly and manipulation; amongst them would be the principle 'Islam does not occasion harm', 'repelling corruption has priority over bringing social good' especially if the corruption is widespread whilst the public good in limited to individuals. Also the principle of 'that which is most important precedes what is less important' and 'the compulsion of protecting the human person'.

And so it is upon Islam and the Muslims to demonstrate that it is the ugliest form for loansharks and opportunistic people who are lurking amongst regular folk (to take advantage of them)."

The holy Qur'an has a number of verses dealing generally and specially about hoarding and prohibiting people from their needs. It also demands just measurement and equitable distribution. When all of these are brought together they portray a clear picture as to God's ﷻ view on withholding from people. Here we will mention a few:

﴿الَّذِينَ يَكْنِزُونَ الذَّهَبَ وَالْفِضَّةَ وَلَا يُنفِقُونَهَا فِي سَبِيلِ اللَّهِ فَبَشِّرْهُم بِعَذَابٍ أَلِيمٍ ﴿٣٤﴾﴾

1. As for all who hoard up treasures of gold and silver and do not spend them for the sake of Gods give them the tiding of grievous suffering. (9:34)

﴿لَا يَكُونَ دُولَةً بَيْنَ الْأَغْنِيَاءِ مِنكُمْ ﴿٧﴾﴾

2. It may not be [a benefit] just going round and round among you as may [already] be rich. (59:7)

﴿فَأَوْفُوا الْكَيْلَ وَالْمِيزَانَ وَلَا تَبْخَسُوا النَّاسَ أَشْيَاءَهُمْ وَلَا تُفْسِدُوا فِي الْأَرْضِ ﴿٨٥﴾﴾

3. Give, therefore, full measure and weight [in all your dealings], and do not deprive people of what is rightfully theirs; and do not spread corruption on earth. (7:85)

﴿يَا أَيُّهَا الَّذِينَ آمَنُواْ كُونُواْ قَوَّامِينَ لِلّهِ شُهَدَاء بِالْقِسْطِ وَلاَ يَجْرِمَنَّكُمْ شَنَآنُ قَوْمٍ عَلَى أَلاَّ تَعْدِلُواْ﴿٨﴾﴾

4. O You who believe! Be ever steadfast in your devotion to God, bearing witness to the truth in all equity; and never let hatred of any-one lead you into the sin of deviating from justice." (5:8)

﴿ٱلَّذِينَ هُمْ عَن صَلَاتِهِمْ سَاهُونَ﴿٥﴾ ٱلَّذِينَ هُمْ يُرَآءُونَ﴿٦﴾ وَيَمْنَعُونَ ٱلْمَاعُونَ﴿٧﴾﴾

5. So woe then to those who want only to be seen and praised and deny and bar even the smallest items [to their fellow-men]!" (107:4-7).

In regard to this last verse, commentators state, the term *ma'un* means 'a little thing'. The purpose of it here is to denote the most insignificant things that some people deny to others, especially their neighbours, like salt, water, matches for fire, dishes, and the like, which are the necessities of life.

Such a person who withholds giving such insignificant things to others is a selfish, miserly, faithless one. These things do not cost too much, but are incredibly helpful, so when they refuse to give or prohibit them, this produces notable difficulties in the lives of people – let alone in a time of heightened need, like a pandemic.

Narrations also detail the grave matter of al-Ihtikar.

The Prophet Muhammad ﷺ said, "Whoever monopolises does not die until Allah afflicts him with disease or bankruptcy" and "In hell there is a specific valley for the monopolisers, those addicted to alcohol and lusts."

In another the Prophet ﷺ states: "Verily the motive of food is to be prosperous and bestowed upon, whilst the monopoliser (by barring that) is accursed."

In this narration is a clear indication that the one who brings in what people need in order to make their lives easier, is in reality the richest person with Allah ﷻ. As for the monopoliser he is the opposite: low, mean and devoid of generosity.

Another narration, from Imam Mohammed al-Baqir ؑ states: "The Messenger of Allah ﷺ said, 'Any person who buys food and withholds it forty days desiring to inflate the price then sells it and gives charity from its profit, there is no expiation of his sin for what he has done.'"

We can conclude from here two important issues: That Islam has addressed the real-world political, economic, social and moral problem of monopolisation of items and their pricing out of availability; and there being a stern warning against this practise, from the most valuable of items such as gold to the minutest like salt. This is because only a selfish, unsympathetic, broken person would withhold or make inaccessible from another knowing their desperation or need for an item. It is clear here that Islam opposes allowing a completely free market, set by those who have access to items, who are able to gobble up the little means and wealth of those who do not have access.

Amongst the Islamic debates is the question, 'Are only essential foods prohibited from being hoarded or does it extend to non-essential food stuffs? What about non-consumables such as electricity or tools or what is locally needed?' This question is necessary to ensure we do not think narrowly about this subject such as confining it to food and water or simply stating it is about high prices and affordability.

Narrations are explicit that needs cannot be based on a shortlist but rather must be relative to time and space.

For example, Imam Ja'far as-Sadiq ﷺ said: "If in the city (place of public services and markets) there was food other than it (what you are used to) then there is no problem (eating what is permissible)"

In another sahih narration he ﷺ said: "If there is a lot of food sufficient for people to get it, then there is no problem."

We can see here relativity in food and location; it is not spoken of in the specific, restricted sense.

The Qur'an also seeks to widen the scope of what people make narrow unnecessarily asking:

> "Who is there to forbid the beauty which God has brought forth for His creatures, and the good things from among the means of sustenance?" (7:32).

The meaning of these narrations and verses is that if monopolising is restricting people then it is the monopolisation that is problematic, not the specific item being monopolised.

The great scholar Muhammad Hasan al-Najafi (d. 1849 AD), known as Sahib al-Jawahir, states: "Monopolisation is prohibited in every category of what is needed by a protected soul and whatever necessity it needs, and not restricted for them in food or water or clothes nor anything else which is restricted to time."

Sheikh Mughniyyah has an emphatic set of statements in these regards: "And we say to the scholars, those who specify the prohibition of monopolisation to wheat and barley and dates, it would necessitate you upon this opinion that the monopolisation of oil and electricity would not be considered prohibited. With certainty, life today would be impossible without these. And also it would necessitate you to monopolise weapons and bar whoever needs to defend himself in a righteous way. What harm comes today if you don't have dates and raisins (compared to not having oil and electricity)?!

And I believe the coloniser, if he were to know about this law – your bowing to the literal meanings and just sticking to the prohibition on dates and raisins and you're allowing monopolisation of iron, steel and gold and this fixed literal meaning (he would exploit it greatly) [and it] is a slander on the *shari'a* of the Master of the Messengers ﷺ."

The debate around what can be prohibited allows us to think broadly about time and space and the relative needs in our own time. During the beginning of the COVID 19 pandemic, the greatest commodity appeared to be antibacterial soaps, hand sanitisers, flour, eggs and the likes. This of course would not be mentioned at the time of Prophet Muhammad ﷺ but is categorised as an essential need today. Therefore it is prohibited from being hoarded, stored for personal gain, or causing harm to others in society by virtue of their lack of access. There are, however, other items which may not be considered essential but people need or want. If by its quantity of purchasing you make it unavailable to people, even though it is not essential but becomes restricted in access, then it too is considered as hoarding and is prohibited.

The way in which Ahl al-Bayt ﷺ acted during a famine or epidemic is not just inspiring but sets the example of how we consider a wholesome and pure response to the challenge of equitable food distribution, such as in the times we live in. It has been mentioned in *Wasai'l as-Shi'a* "In one of the years food had become embargoed to Madinah and people could only buy things on a day by day basis. Imam as-Sadiq ﷺ stated to his workers, "How much food do we have?" "Enough to last us a month" they replied. Imam says "Take it out." "But the city doesn't have food for us to buy" replies the servants. "Sell it!" the Imam commanded. When he sold it (the servant) the Imam said to his servant "Buy food like the people on a day to day basis."

Also mentioned in *Wasai'l as-Shi'a* that the people of Madinah experienced a drought such that even the rich had to mix wheat and barley to survive. And Imam had good food so he said to his servant "Buy for us barley and mix it with the food like people do and sell the good food we have. We dislike to eat well whilst people eat poorly."

Indeed Allah knows the best where to give his message to.

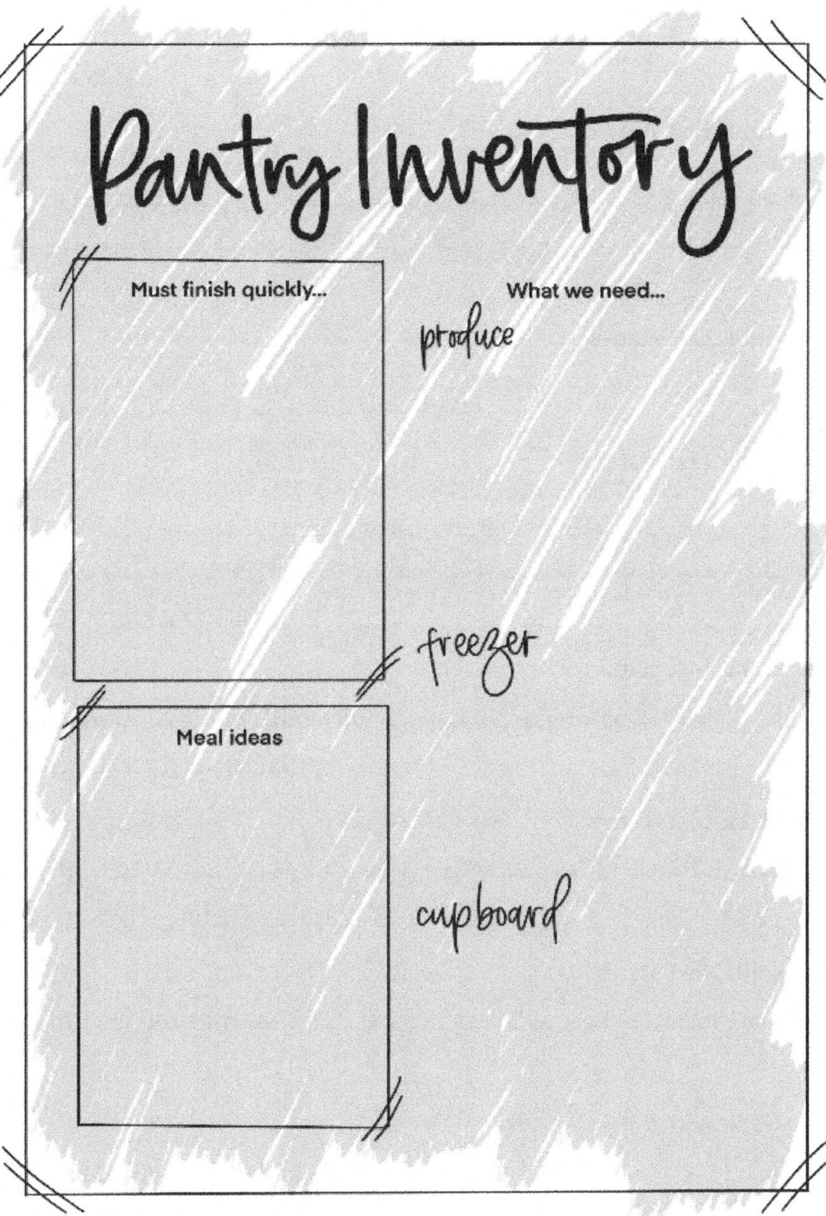
Pantry Inventory
Must finish quickly...
What we need...
produce
freezer
Meal ideas
cupboard

Endnotes

1 The Arabic text states:

ليس في الطعام سرف

2 The Arabic text states:

دعا رجل أمير المؤمنين علي بن أبي طالب، فقال له: أجبت على أن تضمن لي ثلاث خصال، قال: وما هي يا أمير المؤمنين؟ قال: أن لا تدخل عليّ شيئاً من خارج ، ولا تدخر عني شيئاً في البيت ولا تجحف بالعيال

3 The Arabic text states:

ومن احتقر ما يقرب إليه أخوه لم يزل في مقت الله يومه وليلته

4 The Arabic text states:

أكرم أخلاق النبيين والصديقين والشهداء والصالحين التزاور في الله، وحق على المزور أن يقرب إلى أخيه ما تيسر عنده ولو لم يكن إلا جرعة من ماء، فمن احتشم أن يقرب إلى أخيه ما تيسر عنده، لم يزل في مقت الله يومه وليلته

5 The Arabic text states:

من أطعم طعاماً رئاء وسمعة، أطعمه الله من صديد جهنم، وجعل ذلك الطعام ناراً في بطنه حتى يقضي بين الناس يوم القيامة

6 The Arabic text states:

أنه نظر إلى فاكهة قد رميت في داره لم يستقص أكلها فغضب ، فقال: ما هذا؟ إن كنتم شبعتم، فإن كثيراً من الناس لم يشبعوا، فأطعموه من يحتاج إليه

7 The Arabic text states:

أكرموا الخبز، فإن الله تبارك وتعالى انزل له بركات السماء، قيل: وما إكرامه؟ قال: إذا حضر لم ينتظر به غيره

8 The Arabic text states:

صغروا رغافكم، فإن مع كل رغيف بركة

9 Al-Khisal, as-Sadooq, Chapter on the Number Five, Hadith No. 48.

Personal Notes

Chapter Five

Conclusion

Have you ever asked yourself why fast-food chicken are so cheap?

Or why there are so many ubiquitously named fried-chicken shops on the high street, all seemingly named after one U.S. State or another?

In the 1940's America launched a series of "Chicken of Tomorrow" competitions for farmers. The aim, as described by a newspaper at the time, was to produce "one bird chunky enough for the whole family - a chicken with breast meat so thick you can carve it into steaks, with drumsticks that contain a minimum of bone buried in layers of juicy dark meat, all costing less instead of more."

Since then chickens have continued to grow.

A study by Martin Zuidhof of the University of Alberta documented the average size of commercially grown chickens bred in 1957, 1978 and 2005 all at just 56 days old. What they found was staggering: the weights were 0.9kg, then 1.8kg and then 4.2kg across that time span, or four and a half times it pre-industrially produced size.

A vicious cocktail of cheap chicken feed, caged birds trapped with little space for movement, veterinary drugs, growth hormone drugs, environmental pollutants, phytosanitary substances and pesticides keep the chickens growing at 50g per day, something their, immune systems, organs and legs cannot keep pace with.[1] [2]

Sadly, this is not the answer to the question as to why they are so cheap. The real answer is because we continue to consume them. These and the entire system of poor quality food depends on the ignorance of and addiction to cheap, fast food. When we say ignorance we mean falling into the trap of marketing campaigns, for slogans such as 'Farm Fresh' or 'Natural' are meaningless when it comes to animal welfare and quality of product. [3]

It seems with our exponential growth and advancement we have over complicated the simplest of necessary habits, eating. We have created murky waters around the subject of good food. Our greed for more wealth and power has led to confusion, too many choices and a food industry that thrives on quick fixes not without consequences. All of which is leading to the eventual loss of nature's wondrous healing powers.

With the increased awareness of health, increasing demand of healthy food and public discussions on food security the year 2020 should have been a watershed moment; an opportunity for historical global behavioural change.

According to Dr. Stephen Davies, Head of Education at the Institute of Economic Affair's, with current farming practises, we can predictably expect another pandemic to emerge in the next ten or so years for exactly the same reasons.[4]

Despite all of these opportunities for profound systemic change, many restaurateurs describe the shift to delivery apps as an addiction; they know the habit is harming millions of people, but it provides a short-term fix for their profits and so again money comes before health.[5]

From the beginning of time, food has been an essential ingredient to how our human bodies grow, heal and create energy. As we scientifically develop, we have begun to understand the intricate detail and biochemistry of the specific nutrient components that help us function. Science is still only scratching the surface of the universe that God has created within us.

During this 2020 global pandemic we have unveiled the power of nutrients, with Vitamins C and D making major headlines for its surprisingly powerful impact on prevention and reduction in symptoms of COVID-19.[6] [7] The pandemic has awakened the world to the need for optimum health, food habits being a central component of achieving this.

We need to remember that whatever is hailed as being the heroic magic cure, it will never replace the need for us all to be conscious and aware of how we grow, farm, package and eventually eat food. This is the foundation of our health, individually as well as collectively.

There are 10^{31} viruses on earth that we know of, we live in synchrony with these and many species of bacteria. It is only when we change the terrain of our body that we give them the term, foreign invaders. Maintaining a wholefood diet is a major player in sustaining a healthy internal terrain.

To keep things simple what can we do? Return to wholesome ingredients, eat a colourful plate and avoid processed foods. Simple and effective.

Bring back the inquisitive child that loves to know the source of ingredients, the joy of cooking and be thankful for the nourishment that reaches your plate.

Our health, our environment and our future generations are heavily influenced by our decisions and choices. We need to return back to the source of food and the processes that have occurred to bring food to our plate. As an example, as per the organisation Green Peace, up to 12.7 million tonnes of plastic enters the oceans every year, and the equivalent of a truckload of plastic enters the oceans every minute. The broken-down plastics, microplastics, travel in our food chains eventually reaching both animal and human predators. We now know that many of the chemicals from plastic, just like BPA, cause estrogenic effects. They act like the hormone oestrogen, creating havoc with our internal communication signals. In addition, we cannot neglect the ecological devastation that plastic pollution has had on the whole planet.

We can all do our bit to fight against the plastic waste, the first step is being aware of how much we use in our houses. Here are some of the top tips:

- Refuse plastic cutlery
- Did you know that glitter is made up of tiny pieces of plastic?
- Buy a glass mug for your coffees and teas
- Use loose tea leaves as teabags are made of plastic
- Avoid the cling film
- Ditch the chewing gum (it's made with plastic!)
- Count your plastic

God provided us the power to make choices and the power to reverse our wrongs, as He says:

﴿ظَهَرَ ٱلْفَسَادُ فِى ٱلْبَرِّ وَٱلْبَحْرِ بِمَا كَسَبَتْ أَيْدِى ٱلنَّاسِ
لِيُذِيقَهُم بَعْضَ ٱلَّذِى عَمِلُوا۟ لَعَلَّهُمْ يَرْجِعُونَ ٤١﴾

> Corruption has appeared throughout the land and sea by virtue of what men's hands have done that Allah may make them taste some of their deeds in order that they may turn back. (Qur'an 30:41).

The smallest steps that each of us take in becoming more conscious of our food will provide us, our communities and our world with better health, cleaner air and water, less poverty and a thriving ecosystem.

The purpose of this book has been to revive the Islamic social, ethical, economic and spiritual model of the food system and practises of eating. All of these are reliant on each other; when ignorance or greed penetrates one part it necessarily affects the others; when one is undertaken in the consideration of Allah's ﷻ environmental, animal and human rights, it will positively permeate the others.

This demonstrates to us the holistic nature of the the topic of food in Islam and the error of reducing in it anyway. And given its essential role in sustaining life and maximising human potential, its position is at the core of living the Qur'anic vision of *Hayatun Tayyibah*, the purest and most godly form of life.

Ultimately we cannot think of a better narration than the following to summarise the spirit and aim of the book: Prophet Muhammad ﷺ is narrated to have said, "The [true] believer is like the bee; he eats pure *(tayyib)* and produces purity *(tayyib)*. And if he should do something, he would not break [not harm] nor corrupt [not spoil anything]."[8]

We pray and thank the Almighty for creating a world with the potential of making us angelicbeings with the ability to recognise and experience God's beautiful attributes. We ask Allah ﷻ to accept this work and that we can follow its guidance to the best of our abilities.

Endnotes

1 www.economist.com/international/2019/01/19/how-chicken-became-the-rich-worlds-most-popular-meat?

2 www.intechopen.com/books/poultry-science/chemical-contaminants-in-poultry-meat-and-products

3 www.independent.co.uk/life-style/food-and-drink/supermarket-chicken-labels-truth-free-range-battery-treatment-organic-a7751536.html

4 youtu.be/Jr7GeoJv7rI

5 amp.economist.com/1843/2021/01/26/gulp-the-secret-economics-of-food-delivery?

6 orthomolecular.org/resources/omns/v16n42.shtml

7 www.sciencedirect.com/science/article/pii/S0960076020302764?via%3Dihub

8 Hayat al-Hayawan al-Kubra, Kamil ad-Din ad-Damiri, Mu'assassat al-A'lamee LilMatboo'at, Beirut, 2003, vol. 2, pg 421. The Arabic text of this tradition states:

المؤمن كالنحلة تأكل طيباً و تضع طيباً ، و ان وقعت فلم تكسر و لم تفسد

Personal Notes

Works Cited

1. Use of the "Exposome" in the Practice of Epidemiology: A Primer on Omic Technologies. D. Gayle DeBord, Tania Carreón, Thomas J. Lentz, Paul J. Middendorf, Mark D. Hoover, and Paul A. Schulte. s.l. : Am J Epidemiol. , 2017 Aug 15., Vols. 184(4): 302–314.

2. Kresser, Chris. Bone Broth Benefits. [Online] August 16, 2019. www.chriskresser.com/benefits-of-bone-broth-a-comprehensive-guide.

3. Oregano: A potential prophylactic treatment for the intestinal microbiota. Benjamin W. Bauer, Anita Radovanovic, Nicky-Lee Willson, Yadav Sharma Bajagai, Thi Thu Hao Van, Robert J. Moore, and Dragana Stanleya,*. s.l. : Heliyon, 2019 Oct, Vol. 5(10).

4. Understanding the Impact of Omega-3 Rich Diet on the Gut Microbiota. Blanca S. Noreiga, Marcos A. Sanchez Gonzalez, Daria Salyakina, and Jonathan Coffman. s.l. : Case Reports Medicine, 2016.

5. Nut consumption in relation to cardiovascular disease risk and type 2 diabetes: a systematic review and meta-analysis of prospective studies. Zhou D, Yu H, He F, Reilly KH, et al. s.l. : Am J

Clin Nutr., 2014 May 7, Vols. 100(1):270-277.

6. Effects of the intestinal microbial metabolite butyrate on the development of colorectal cancer. Xinqiang Wu, Yuanbing Wu, Liangmei He, Longhuo Wu, Xiangcai Wang, and Zhiping Liu. 2510–2517, s.l. : J Cancer., 2018, Vol. 9(14).

7. Association between eating behaviour and diet quality: eating alone vs. eating with others. Wonjeong Chae, Yeong Jun Ju, Jaeyong Shin, Sung-In Jang & Eun-Cheol Park. s.l. : Nutrition Journal , 2018 , Vols. volume 17, Article number: 117.

8. —.Wonjeong Chae, Yeong Jun Ju, Jaeyong Shin, Sung-In Jang, and Eun-Cheol Park. s.l. : Nutr J., 2018, Vol. 17: 117.

9. Organic foods contain higher levels of certain nutrients, lower levels of pesticides, and may provide health benefits for the consumer. WJ., Crinnion. s.l. : Altern Med Rev. 2010, 2010 Apr, Vols. 15(1):4-12.

10. Beneficial effects of polyphenol-rich olive oil in patients with early atherosclerosis. Widmer RJ, Freund MA, Flammer AJ, Sexton J, et al. s.l. : Eur J Nutr, 2012 Aug.

11. WHO. Definition of Health. World Health Organisation. [Online] April 7, 1948. https://www.who.int/about/who-we-are/constitution.

12. —. Chronic Diseases. Chronic Disease. [Online] [Cited: April 12, 2020.] The burden of chronic diseases is rapidly increasing worldwide. It has been calculated that, in 2001, chronic diseases contributed approximately 60% of the 56.5 million total reported

deaths in the world and approximately 46% of the global burden of disea.

13. Peer review under review: room for improvement? Wall, E.E. van der. s.l. : Neth Heart J, 2009 May, Vol. 17(5): 187.

14. Mediterranean diet and age-related cognitive decline: a randomized clinical trial. Valls-Pedret C, Sala-Vila A, Serra-Mir M, Corella D, et al. doi: 10.1001/jamainternmed.2015.1668., s.l. : JAMA Intern Med., 2015 Jul, Vols. 175(7):1094-103.

15. Role of the gut microbiota in nutrition and health. Valdes, Ana M. 361, s.l. : BMJ ; , 2018.

16. UK, Cancer Research. Cancer Statistics. Cancer Statistics. [Online] [Cited: April 12, 2020.] https://www.cancerresearchuk.org/health-professional/cancer-statistics.

17. Eating Alone Yet Living With Others Is Associated With Mortality in Older Men: The JAGES Cohort Survey. Tani Y, Kondo N, Noma H, Miyaguni Y, Saito M, Kondo K. s.l. : J Gerontol B Psychol Sci Soc Sci., 2018 Sep, Vols. 20;73(7)1330-1334.

18. Relationships of dietary patterns, foods, and micro and macronutrients with alzheimer's disease and late-life cognitive disorders: a systematic review. Solfrizzi V, Cus-todero C, Lozupone M, Imbimbo BP, et al. doi: 10.3233/JAD-170248., s.l. : J Alzheimers Dis., 2017, Vols. 59(3):815-849.

19. Peer review: a flawed process at the heart of science and journals. Smith, Richard. s.l. : J R Soc Med. , 2006 Apr, Vols. 99(4): 178–182.

20. Effect of agronomical practices on carpology, fruit and oil composition, and oil sensory properties, in olive. Rosati A, Cafiero C, Paoletti A, Alfei B, et al. s.l. : Food Chem., 2014 Sep 15, Vols. 159:236-43. doi: 10.1016/j.

21. Eating attentively: a systematic review and meta-analysis of the effect of food intake memory and awareness on eating. Robinson E1, Aveyard P, Daley A, Jolly K, Lewis A, Lycett D, Higgs S. s.l. : Am J Clin Nutr. , 2013 Apr, Vols. 97(4):728-42. doi: 10.3945/ajcn.112.045245.

22. Effect of the mediterranean diet on cognition and brain morphology and function: a systematic review of randomized controlled trials. Radd-Vagenas S, Duffy SL, Naismith SL, Brew BJ, et al. s.l. : Am J Clin Nutr., 2018 Mar 1, Vols. (3):389-404. doi: 10.1093/ajcn/nqx070.

23. Publications, Ansaryian. Islamic Medical Wisdom - Tibb Al Aimma. s.l. : Ansaryian Publications https://www.al-islam.org/islamic-medical-wisdom-tibb-al-aimma.

24. Role of walnuts in maintaining brain health with age. Poulose SM, Miller MG, Shukitt-Hale B. 2014 Apr, J Nutr., pp. 144 (4 Suppl): 561S-566S. doi: 10.3945/jn.113.184838.

25. Maternal high-fat diet in mice programs emotional behavior in adulthood. Peleg-Raibstein D1, Luca E, Wolfrum C. doi: 10.1016/j.bbr.2012.05.027, s.l. : Behav Brain Res., 2012 Aug 1;, Vols. 233(2):398-404.

26. Comparison of nutritional quality between conventional and organic dairy products: a meta-analysis. Palupi E, Jayanegara A,

Ploeger A, Kahl J. s.l. : J Sci Food Agric., 2012 Nov, Vols. 92(14):2774-81. doi: 10.1002/jsfa.5639.

27. Maternal overnutrition leads to cognitive and neurochemical abnormalities in C57BL/6 mice. Paleg-Raibstein, Christian Wolfrum and Daria. Issue 10, s.l. : Journal Nutritional Neuroscience, 2019, Vol. Volume 22.

28. Organization, World Health. Noncommunicable Diseases. [Online] [Cited: April 12, 2020.] https://www.who.int/news-room/fact-sheets/detail/noncommunicable-diseases.

29. NASA. Evidence for Global Warming. NASA Climate Change Evidence . [Online] [Cit-ed: April 12, 2020.] https://climate.nasa.gov/evidence/.

30. Moss, Michael. Salt, Sugar, Fat: How the Food Giants Hooked Us. s.l. : Random House Publishing Group, 2013.

31. Medicine, Institute of Functional. Institute of Functional Medicine. ifm. [Online] www.ifm.org.

32. Secoiridoids delivered as olive leaf extract induce acute improvements in human vas-cular function and reduction of an inflammatory cytokine: a randomised, double-blind, placebo-controlled, cross-over trial. Lockyer S, Corona G, Yaqoob P, Spencer JP, Rowland I. 2015 Jul 14, Br J Nutr., pp. 114(1):75-83. doi: 10.1017/S0007114515001269.

33. Fatty acids and their therapeutic potential in neurological disorders. Lei E, Vacy K, Boon WC. 2016 May, Neurochem Int., pp. 95:75-84. doi: 10.1016/j.neuint.2016.02.014.

34. The gut microbiome and the brain. L., Galland. doi: 10.1089/jmf.2014.7000, s.l. : J Med Food., 2014 Dec, Vols. 17(12):1261-72.

35. Eating alone and metabolic syndrome: A population-based Korean National Health and Nutrition Examination Survey 2013-2014. Kwon AR, Yoon YS, Min KP, Lee YK, Jeon JH. s.l. : Obes Res Clin Pract., 2018 Mar - Apr, Vols. 12(2):146-157. doi: 10.1016/j.orcp.2017.09.002.

36. Stress and the gut: pathophysiology, clinical consequences, diagnostic approach and treatment options. Konturek PC, Brzozowski T, Konturek SJ. s.l. : J Physiol Pharmacol., 2011 Dec, Vols. 62(6):591-9.

37. Probable carcinogenicity of glyphosate. Kogevinas, Manolis. s.l. : BMJ , 2019, Vol. 365 doi: https://doi.org/10.1136/bmj.l1613.

38. Khomeini, Sayyid Ruhullah Musawi. Recommendations for the Seminaries of Religious Learning. Jihad Al Akbar, The Greatest Jihad: Combat the Self. s.l. : The Institute for the Compilation and Publication of the Works of Imam Khomeini.

39. Health benefits of almonds beyond cholesterol reduction. Kamil A, Chen CY. 2012 Jul, J Agric Food Chem., pp. 60(27):6694-702. doi: 10.1021/jf2044795.

40. Meat quality and health implications of organic and conventional beef production. Kamihiro S, Stergiadis S, Leifert C, Eyre MD, Butler G. s.l. : Meat Sci., 2015 Feb, Vols. 100:306-18.

41. Indigenous bacteria from the gut microbiota regulate host serotonin biosynthesis. Jessica M. Yano, 1 Kristie Yu,1 Gregory P.

Donaldson,1 Gauri G. Shastri, Phoebe Ann, Liang Ma, Cathryn R. Nagler, Rustem F. Ismagilov, Sarkis K. Mazmanian, and Elaine Y. Hsiao. 264–276, s.l. : Cell., 2015 Apr 9, Vol. 161(2).

42. Imam Musa Al-Kadhim, (a.s). P180, s.l. : Makarim Al-Akhlaq, Vol. 2. No. 2,468.

43. Maintaining gut homeostasis: The butyrate–NF-κB connection. Hodin, Richard. Issue 4, s.l. : Gastroentrology, April 2000, Vol. Volume 118. Pages 798–801.

44. Dietary fats and health: dietary recommendations in the context of scientific evidence. GD., Lawrence. 2013, Adv Nutr., pp. 4(3):294-302. doi: 10.3945/an.113.003657.

45. The role of dietary coconut for the prevention and treatment of Alzheimer's disease: potential mechanism of action. Fernando WM, Martins IJ, Goozee KG, Brennan CS, et al. 2015 Jul 14, Br J Nutr., pp. 114(1):1-14. doi: 10.1017.

46. All disease begins in the (leaky) gut: role of zonulin-mediated gut permeability in the pathogenesis of some chronic inflammatory diseases. Fasano, Alessio. s.l. : F1000Res., 2020 Jan 31.

47. Eating attentively: a systematic review and meta-analysis of the effect of food intake memory and awareness on eating. Eric Robinson, Paul Aveyard, Amanda Daley, Kate Jolly, Amanda Lewis, Deborah Lycett, Suzanne Higgs. Issue 4 , s.l. : The American Journal of Clinical Nutrition,, April 2013, Vols. Volume 97,. Pages 728–742.

48. Emoto, Masaru. The Hidden Messages In Water. s.l. : Scribner, 2005.

49. Hass avocado composition and potential health effects. Dreher ML, Davenport AJ. 2013, Crit Rev Food Sci Nutr., pp. 53(7):738-50. doi: 10.1080/10408398.2011.556759.

50. The evidence of human exposure to glyphosate: a review. Christina Gillezeau, Maaike van Gerwen, Rachel M. Shaffer, Iemaan Rana, Luoping Zhang, Lianne Sheppard & Emanuela Taioli. 2, s.l. : Environmental Health, 2019, Vol. 18.

51. Bray, Natasha. The microbiota–gut–brain axis. The microbiotagut–brain axis. [Online] JUNE 17, 2019. [Cited: April 16, 2020.] https://www.nature.com/articles/d42859-019-00021-3.

52. Diet-induced cognitive deficits: the role of fat and sugar, potential mechanisms and nutritional interventions. Beilharz JE, Maniam J, Morris MJ. doi: 10.3390/nu7085307, s.l. : Nutrients, 2015 Aug 12, Vols. 7(8):6719-38.

53. BBC. Weedkiller glyphosate a 'substantial' cancer factor. Weedkiller glyphosate a 'substantial' cancer factor. [Online] https://www.bbc.co.uk/news/business-47633086.

54. Higher antioxidant and lower cadmium concentrations and lower incidence of pesticide residues in organically grown crops: a systematic literature review and meta-analyses. Barański M, Srednicka-Tober D, Volakakis N, Seal C, et al. s.l. : Br J Nutr. , 2014 Sep 14, Vols. 112(5):794-811. doi: 10.1017/S0007114514001366.

55. Dietary patterns and cognition in older persons. Abbatecola AM, Russo M, Barbieri M. doi: 10.1097/MCO.0000000000000434, s.l. : Curr Opin Clin Nutr Metab, 2018 Jan, Vols. 21(1):10-13.

56. Toxic Chemicals Enquiry. [Online] Feb 2019. https://www.parliament.uk/business/committees/committees-a-z/commons-select/environmental-audit-committee/news-parliament-2017/toxic-chemicals-inquiry-launched-17-19/

Made in United States
Orlando, FL
09 March 2025

59304907R00104